Study Guide for
THE ENJOYMENT
OF MUSIC
THIRD EDITION

BY

RUBIN BERGREEN

Associate Professor of Music, Queens College
of the City University of New York

AND

JOHN CASTELLINI

Professor Emeritus, Queens College of the City University of New York

W · W · NORTON & COMPANY · INC · *New York*

ISBN 0 393 09932 6

The painting on the cover is Juan Gris' *Le Violon* (Kunstmuseum, Basel; permission A.D.A.G.P. 1969 by French Reproduction Rights Inc.; courtesy of Colorphoto Hinz, Basel).

PRINTED IN THE UNITED STATES OF AMERICA

6 7 8 9 0

Foreword

This Study Guide is based on *The Enjoyment of Music*, Third Edition, by Joseph Machlis. The materials in the Study Guide:

1. Focus upon, extract, and assimilate the salient aspects of the text.
2. Assist the student in acquiring a music vocabulary.
3. Offer the student a means of orientation and self-examination in regard to the subject matter in the text.
4. Broaden the student's musical horizon through guided listening and analysis of compositions of various types.
5. Develop a technique of disciplined listening whereby the student can learn to recognize and evaluate musical procedures, principles of structure, and aspects of style.
6. Give direction to perceptive listening and lead the student toward a total musical experience through increased understanding.

The Study Guide is organized as follows:

1. *Short-answer questions* and *statements* based on the principal substance in designated chapters.
2. *Charts* and *outlines* designed to highlight the characteristics of the outstanding periods in music.
3. *Guided listening* in the field of abstract music.
4. *Aural analyses* of (a) elements of music, (b) musical structures and textures, (c) stylistic characteristics of diverse periods, and (d) components of opera.
5. *General review* for each part of the text.
6. *Forms* for biographical sketches and stylistic evaluations.

In its organization, the Study Guide reflects the same flexibility of application that is inherent in the parent text. Neither presents restrictions; neither inflicts set patterns; neither requires revision of one's philosophy or methodology in teaching music appreciation. The procedural sequence of the Study Guide is identical with that of the text and allows the same freedom of approach to the subject. As with the parent text, the teacher may choose whatever chronological order he prefers.

The material presented in the individual *Study Guides*, related *Charts, Outlines,* and *General Reviews* may be utilized in a flexible manner to suit individual class needs.

Separate portions of the *Study Guide* may be used in a variety of ways:

    a) In-class discussions
    b) Out-of-class assignments
    c) Testing

The Study Guide stresses musical concepts, musical values, and the musical experience. "A work of art embodies a view of life. It brings us the artist's personal interpretation of human destiny, the essence of his experience both as artist and man. In order to comprehend the work we must enter the secret world out of which it sprang. *The greater our understanding, the better we capture the joy, the illumination that went into its making.*" (Chapter 1.) The Study Guide is designed to bring to the student this greater understanding; its ultimate objective is *the enjoyment of music.*

The authors wish to thank David Hamilton and to acknowledge with deep appreciation his concerned and expert guidance in the publication of this work.

Rubin Bergreen
John Castellini

Note

The following general directions should be observed.

1. *Incomplete statements* should be filled in with appropriate words or phrases as indicated.
2. *Charts* and *Outlines* should be completed as instructed.
3. Where they differ in two versions, references are given as follows: R = Regular Version, S = Shorter Version.
4. Items preceded by an asterisk (*) are for use with the Regular Version only.

LISTENING GUIDES AND AURAL ANALYSIS OUTLINES

TO THE TEACHER AND STUDENT

These charts are intended to aid the student in the process of perceptive listening by focusing attention on musical materials and procedures. Since the purpose is to *assist* the listener and not to examine him, the following is suggested: *on the blackboard, or with flash-card, show — prior to the moment it occurs — the number that applies to the musical event being considered.*

INSTRUCTIONS FOR USE OF LISTENING GUIDES

1. Every statement in the Listening Guides refers to an event in the music. Before listening, familiarize yourself with each Guide.
2. As you listen, follow the Guide. Note the structural outline as the music progresses, using the listed musical features as "landmarks" or "guideposts".

INSTRUCTIONS FOR USE OF AURAL ANALYSIS OUTLINES

1. Familiarize yourself with each Outline.
2. Listen to each movement for general impression.
3. Listen again and check the appropriate description of each designated musical event as it occurs.

APPENDIX

The Appendix contains:
1. Bar references to Listening Guides
2. Supplementary Outlines:
    a) Biographical Sketch
    b) Absolute Music Analysis — Eighteenth-Nineteenth Centuries
    c) Stylistic Evaluation — Baroque
    d) Aural Analysis — Stylistic Evaluation (Twentieth Century)

Part One

THE MATERIALS OF MUSIC

Study Guide 1

The following incomplete statements are derived from the text. Find the quotations and complete each with the author's words.

CHAPTER I

1. "To listen perceptively requires that we
   a) fasten our whole attention upon the sounds as they came floating thru the air.
   b) observe the patterns they form.
   c) respond to the thought and feeling out of which those patterns have emerged."

2. "Music as an art bases its appeal on the sensuous beauty of musical sounds."

3. "..., whatever brings him (the listener) closer to the sounds heightens his musical perception and his enjoyment."

4. "... music, like language, aims to communicate meaning."

5. "It will heighten our perception (of music) if we know something about the elements of which music is composed, and the way that composers go about organizing tones into patterns and forms. We may inquire into the forces that have shaped musical activity at various periods, the school & movements within the art and their relationship to the social environment. We should have some knowledge of the men whose genius enriched the lives of their fellows, of their style, and of their contribution to the art."

6. "Music is an art dealing with the organization of tones into patterns.

CHAPTER 2

1. "A number of theories have been advanced to explain [music's] origin." List eight such theories:
   a) *inflections of speech*   e) *imitation of nature*
   b) *mating calls*   f) *play impulse*
   c) *cries of battle + the hunt*   g) *magic + religious rites*
   d) *rhythms of collective labor*   h) *need for emotional expression*

2. "We have in .... a treasury of song that reflects ...."
   List ten types of folk songs:
   a) *work songs*   f) *dance songs*
   b) *love "*   g) *songs of mourning*
   c) *drinking "*   h) *marching songs*
   d) *cradle "*   i) *play "*
   e) *patriotic "*   j) *narrative "*

3. "A dance piece may be intended for actual use in the *ballroom* . Or a dance rhythm may serve as the basis for an *abstract composition* ...."

4. "March rhythm may serve too as the basis for an *abstract piece* ...."

5. "The religious impulse has motivated *a considerable amount of the world's great music* . Most works in this category were composed expressly for use in the *church service* ; others are *concert pieces* on sacred themes."

6. "The *opera* forms another potent link between *life* and *music* ."

Due Sept 3

Study Guide 2

CHAPTER 3

1. A *melody* is a succession of single tones perceived as a unity.

2. A phrase ends in a kind of resting place called a *cadence*.

3. Three ways in which the character of a melody may be determined:

    a) Unity and variety are achieved through *repitition* and *contrast*.

    b) In addition to repeated tones, a melodic phrase may move in an *upward* or *downward* line.

    c) Its forward motion in time is determined by its *rhythm*.

4. The Latin word *Opus* together with a number indicates the order of composition or publication in a composer's output.

— (should be in this order)

CHAPTER 4

1. The distance and relationship between two tones is called an *interval*.

2. The element of music that pertains to the movement and relationship of intervals and chords is called *harmony*.

3. A single harmonic unit of three or more tones is called a *chord*.

4. Melody constitutes the *horizontal* aspect of music; *harmony*, the vertical.

                                                     Check (✔)

5. In the following example, the melody is on staff   a) ✔   b) ....

                       the chords are on staff   a) ....   b) ✔

6. A chord of rest is counterposed to chords which are *active*.

7. Active chords seek to be *resolved* in a rest chord.

8. Underline the correct completions:

    a) A chord that imparts a sense of tension and activity is referred to as

        Consonant   <u>Dissonant</u>

    b) A chord that imparts a sense of rest and fulfillment is referred to as

        <u>Consonant</u>   Dissonant

9. With respect to consonance and dissonance, music has grown more *dissonant* through the ages.

3

CHAPTER 5

1. In the most general sense, the element related to the controlled movement of music in time is *rhythm*

2. The aspect of rhythm concerned with regularly recurring groups of beats (fixed time patterns) is called
   meter.

3. A metrical unit of time (a group of beats) containing a primary (strong) accent is called a *measure*

4. The *first* beat of the measure generally receives the strongest accent.

5. List the four most common meters and indicate the number of beats per measure:

   a) *2/4* meter has *2* beats per measure.

   b) *3/4 3/2* meter has *3* beats per measure.

   c) *4/4* meter has *4* beats per measure.

   d) *6/8 6/4* meter has *6* beats per measure.

6. The shifting of an accent from a strong to a weak beat is called *syncopation*.

METER RECOGNITION

1. Sing or play the following melodies. Determine the location of the primary accent. Count the total number of pulses (beats) which occur from one primary accent to the next. Identify, with the number 2 or 3, those tunes which may be considered in the general category of *duple* (or its multiple) or *triple* meter.

		METER
a)	*Did You Ever See a Lassie?* (sing the books of Moses)	3
b)	*Mary Had a Little Lamb*	2
c)	*Happy Birthday*	3
d)	*I've Been Working on the Railroad*	2

2. Identify the meter in each of the following pieces and/or others of your choice:

		METER
a)	Grieg: *Peer Gynt* Suite No. 1 (Excerpts)	
	The Death of Åse (Andante doloroso)	4/4
	Anitra's Dance (Tempo di Mazurka)	3/4
b)	Bizet: *Carmen*, Prelude to Act I (Allegro giocoso)	2/2
c)	*Prokofiev: Three Oranges Suite : March*	
d)		
e)		

Study Guide 3

CHAPTER 6

1. That element of music which reflects the rate of speed of the beats is called .... *Tempo* ....

2. Match the tempo terms in Column II to those in Column I:

		COLUMN I	COLUMN II
a)	*largo*	Broad (very slow)	Accelerando
b)	*adagio*	Quite slow	Adagio
c)	*andante*	A walking pace	Allegretto
d)	*allegretto*	Moderately fast	Allegro
e)	*allegro*	Fast (cheerful)	Andante
f)	*presto*	Very fast	A tempo
g)	*prestissimo*	Very, very fast	Largo
h)	*accelerando*	Getting faster	Prestissimo
i)	*ritardando*	Getting slower	Presto
j)	*a tempo*	Return to original speed	Ritardando

TEMPO RECOGNITION

1. Using the terms *adagio*, *allegro*, *andante*, and *presto*, identify the basic tempo in each of the following pieces and/or others of your choice:

   a) Mozart: Symphony No. 39 in E-Flat — 4th movement (Duple Meter)   *allegro*

   b) Mozart: *Haffner Symphony* # 35 — 2nd movement (Duple Meter)   *Andante*

   c) Beethoven: String Quartet, Op. 130 — Cavatina (Triple Meter)   ....

   d) Mendelssohn: *Italian Symphony* — 4th movement (Quadruple Meter)   *presto*

   e) ....

   f) ....

   g) ....

2. Using the terms *accelerando* and *ritardando*, identify the progressive change(s) in tempo in the following pieces and/or others of your choice:

   a) Grieg: *Peer Gynt* Suite No. 1 — *In the Hall of the Mountain King*   *accel - rit*

   b) Schumann: ~~Dichterliebe~~ *Frauenliebe und Leben : III* — No. 1, *Im wunderschönen Monat Mai* (final measures)   *ritardando*

   c) Verdi: *La Traviata* — Prelude (Final measures)   ....

   d) Johann Strauss: *Die Fledermaus* — Overture (Opening section)   ....

   e) *Berlioz: Symphony Fantastique : V*   *rit - accel*

   f) ....

CHAPTER 7

1. The general term that refers to the degree of loudness and softness in music is _dynamics_

2. Match the terms in Column II to those in Column I:

	COLUMN I	COLUMN II	
a) _pianissimo_	Very soft	crescendo	(◁)
b) _piano_	Soft	decrescendo or diminuendo	(▷)
c) _mezzo piano_	Moderately soft	forte	(f)
d) _mezzo forte_	Moderately loud	fortissimo	(ff)
e) _forte_	Loud	mezzo forte	(mf)
f) _fortissimo_	Very loud	mezzo piano	(mp)
g) _crescendo_	Growing louder	pianissimo	(pp)
h) _decrescendo_	Growing softer	piano	(p)
i) _sforzando_	Sudden stress or accent	sforzando	(sf)

DYNAMICS RECOGNITION

Using the abbreviations p and f, identify the predominant level of dynamics in the opening measures of the following pieces and/or others of your choice:

	DYNAMICS
a) Respighi: *The Pines of Rome* — 1st movement	_loud_
b) Verdi: *Aïda* — Triumphal March	
c) Prokofiev: *Classical Symphony* — 2nd movement	_p_
d) Tchaikovsky: *Nutcracker Suite* — Arab Dance	_p_
e) Tchaikovsky: *Nutcracker Suite* — Russian Dance	
f) _4th Sym: IV_	_f_
g) _Debussy: Prelude_	_mp_

RECOGNITION OF CHANGES IN DYNAMICS

Using the appropriate abbreviations or symbols [*dim.* (▷) and/or *cresc.* (◁)], identify the progressive changes in dynamics in the following pieces and/or others of your choice. If a composition contains both (*dim.* and *cresc.*), indicate accordingly.

	DYNAMICS CHANGES
a) Rossini: *Semiramide* — Overture (Opening)	
b) Verdi: Requiem Mass — *Dies irae* (1st 90 bars)	
c) Wagner: *The Flying Dutchman* — Overture (1st 64 bars)	
d) Verdi: *La Traviata* — Act 1, Chorus: *Si ridesta in ciel l'aurora*	
e) Tchaikovsky: Violin Concerto — 1st movement (opening)	
f) _Beethoven: Piano Sonata in C minor Op. 13: I_	
g)	

6

Study Guide 4

CHAPTERS 8, 9

On the following chart, list the instruments of the orchestra. List the string, woodwind, and brass instruments in order of range — from highest to lowest.

STRING SECTION

WOODWIND SECTION

	PRINCIPAL INSTRUMENT	AUXILIARY INSTRUMENT	CHECK (✔) SINGLE REED	DOUBLE REED	NO REED
Violin	flute	piccolo			✔
Viola	oboe	Eng. Horn		✔	
Cello	clarinet	bass clarinet	✔		
Bass	bassoon	contrabassoon		✔	

BRASS SECTION

INSTRUMENT	CHECK (✔) SLIDE	VALVES
Trumpet		✔
French Horn		✔
Trombone	✔	
Tuba		✔

PERCUSSION SECTION

TUNED INSTRUMENTS (DEFINITE PITCH)	UNTUNED INSTRUMENTS (INDEFINITE PITCH)
Timpani	snare drum
Glockenspiel	tenor drum
Celeste	Bass drum
Xylophone	Tom-Tom
Marimba	Tambourine
Vibraphone	Castanets
Chimes	Triangle
	Cymbals
	Gong

OTHER INSTRUMENTS

INSTRUMENT	FEATURES
saxophone	Single-reed; conical tube; metal body (p. 35)
harp	Strings; pedals; not bowed
piano	Keyboard; strings; hammers; pedals;
organ	Keyboard; pipes; wind; pedals

1. The distinctive tone quality of an instrument that differentiates its sound from that of other instruments is called ....timbre..........

2. A specific area (low, middle, or high) in the range of an instrument or voice is called a .....register.....

3. Four properties of musical sound are:

   a) ....pitch.... b) ....duration.... c) ....volume.... d) ....color....

4. Pitch refers to the location of a tone in relation to ....high......... and ....low.... frequencies.

5. Supply the terms that indicate kinds of tonal articulation commonly associated with string instruments:

   a) Plucking the string ....pizzicato................

   b) A throbbing effect achieved by a rapid wrist-and-finger movement slightly altering the pitch ....vibrato..........

   c) The rapid repetition of a tone through a quick up-and-down movement of the bow ....tremolo..........

   d) Playing simultaneously on two strings ....double-stopping..........

   e) Tones in the very high register produced by lightly touching the string at certain points while the bow is drawn across the string ....harmonics..........

6. Supply the terms that indicate kinds of tonal articulation associated with most melody-producing instruments:

   a) Smooth and connected ....legato..........

   b) Short and detached ....staccato..........

   c) A rapid (slide-like) sounding of all the pitches of the scale ....glissando..........

   d) A rapid alternation between a tone and its neighbor ....trill..........

   e) A device used to muffle and change sound ....mute..........

   f) A manner of playing the tones of a chord one after the other instead of simultaneously (p. 41) ....arpeggio..........

CHAPTER 10

1. The typical orchestra of Bach's day (1685-1750) numbered approximately .....20..... players.

2. The typical orchestra of Mozart's day (1756-1791) numbered approximately .....40..... players.

3. The modern orchestra numbers approximately .....100+..... players.

4. The instrumental and/or vocal parts of a musical composition, written out on individual staves arranged vertically one above the other comprise the .....score.....

5. The art of setting music for instrumental combinations is called .....orchestration.....

6. An instrumental work consisting of a number of complete pieces (movements) related to a central idea is called a .....suite.....

7. A rhythmic or melodic pattern repeated persistently is called .....ostinato.....

8. A solo passage within an orchestral work designed to display the virtuosity of the performer and the capacities of the instrument is called a .....cadenza.....

8

Study Guide 5

Re-read Chapter 3, *The Structure of Melody.*

CHAPTER 11

1. In order to project its intended meaning, an art work must have some plan and organization. This structural aspect of art is referred to as ...*form*...............................

2. The two basic qualities of musical form that are manifested in sameness and difference through repetition and contrast are .....*unity*.............. and ......*variety*..............

3. A basic type of musical form whose structure is planned on the principle of statement-departure-return is called ......*ternary*...... *(A B A)*...... form.

4. Ternary form is commonly represented by the letters ......*A*...., ...*B*...., ...*A*.....

5. Check those letter combinations that represent the statement-departure-return principle in musical form:

   ......✓...... a-b-a   .... a-b-b

   .... a-a-b   ......✓...... a-(a)-b-a

6. The concluding section of a composition is called the ....*coda*........................

7. A basic type of musical structure comprising two parts, the second of which constitutes a contrast to the first, is called ......*binary*.................... form.

8. Binary form is commonly represented by the letters ......*A*...., ...*B*......

9. The distinguishing characteristic of binary form: section ....*A*................ does not return after the completion of section ....*B*..............

10. The distinguishing characteristic of ternary form: section ....*A*.......... returns after the completion of section ....*B*...............

CHAPTER 12

1. The characteristic manner of presentation in any art is called ....*style*.................

2. Supply the appropriate dates for the following style periods in music:

   Renaissance ......*1450*...... - ......*1600*......
   Baroque ......*1600*...... - ......*1750*......
   Classical ......*1775*...... - ......*1825*......
   Romantic ......*1820*...... - ......*1900*......

end Worksheet assignment # 1

FORM RECOGNITION

1. Listen for: a) Statement of the initial musical idea
   b) Contrasting section
   c) Possible restatement of the initial musical idea
2. On the chart, check the similar and contrasting musical sections in the order of their appearance.
3. *Identify the form* of each composition and/or others of your choice.

FORM-ANALYSIS CHART

	SECTIONS: CHECK (✔)			FORM: CHECK (✔)	
	STATEMENT	DEPARTURE	RETURN	BINARY	TERNARY
1. a) *Home on the Range* (Cowboy Song)	✔	✔	✔		✔
b) *America* (Carey)	✔	✔		✔	
c) *America the Beautiful* (Ward)	✔	✔		✔	
d) *Oh! Susanna* (Foster)					
2. a) Tchaikowsky: *Nutcracker Suite —* *Russian Dance* #1	✔	✔	✔		✔
b) Beethoven: Piano Sonata No. 23 in F minor, Op. 57 — 2nd movement, Theme only	*a a* ✔	*b b*		✔	
c) Beethoven: Contradance No. 1					
d) Beethoven: Sonata No. 5 in F major for Violin and Piano, Op. 24 — 3rd movement					
e) Schubert: Piano Quintet in A major, Op. 114 (*Trout*) — 4th movement, Theme only	✔	✔		✔	
f) Glazunov: *The Seasons — Autumn* (*Bacchanale*)					
g)					
h)					
i)					
j)					

Study Guide 6

CHAPTER 13

1. The duration of musical sound is represented graphically by a system of symbols called *notes* ....
....

2. The name given to the following arrangement of lines and spaces

   is *staff* .

3. The name of this symbol  is *Treble clef sign* .

4. The name of this symbol 𝄢 is *bass clef sign* .

5. The combination 𝄞 forms the *Treble clef* which indicates a specific range of pitches above middle C.

6. The combination 𝄢 forms the *bass clef* which indicates a specific range of pitches below middle C.

7. On the following great (grand) staff, write the letter names appropriate to the lines and spaces. Begin with the bottom line and proceed, from left to right, to the top line.

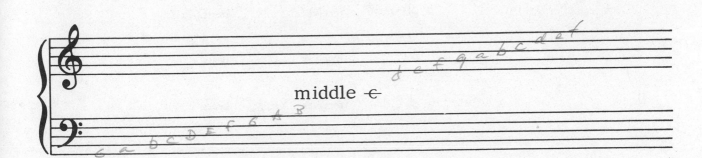

middle c

8. Musical signs used to indicate that the pitch of a note should be altered are called *accidentals* .

9. Identify the following accidentals and describe their function.:

♯   _sharp   raise ½ step_

♭   _flat   lower ½ step_

♮   _natural   cancels ♯ or ♭_

10. The time values of two successive notes of the same pitch may be combined by the use of a _tie_

11. The duration of a note may be extended by one-half its own time value by the use of a _dot_

12. The duration of silence is indicated by symbols called _rests_

13. The numerical symbol that specifies the meter is called _time signatures_

14. In common ($\frac{4}{4}$) time:

𝅝   receives ..._4_... beats.

𝅗𝅥   receives ..._2_... beats.

♩   receives ..._1_... beat.

♪   receives ..._½_... beat.

♬   receives ..._¼_... beat.

15. In $\frac{6}{8}$ time:

♪   receives ..._1_... beat.

♩   receives ..._2_... beats.

♩.   receives ..._3_... beats.

𝅗𝅥.   receives ..._6_... beats.

16. As a rule, the bar line is followed by the beat with the strongest ..._accent_...

General Review I. The Materials of Music

Match each item in Column II to its appropriate association in Column I:

	COLUMN I	COLUMN II
1. *melody*	A succession of single tones perceived as a unity	Cadence
2. *Cadence*	A kind of resting place that ends a phrase	Chord
3. *Harmony*	The element of music that pertains to the movement and relationships of intervals and chords	Consonance
4. *Interval*	The distance and relationship between two tones	Dissonance
5. *Chord*	A single harmonic unit of three or more tones	Duple Meter
6. *Dissonance*	The quality in harmony that imparts a sense of tension and activity	Dynamics
7. *Consonance*	The quality in harmony that imparts a sense of rest and fulfillment	Harmony
8. *Rhythm*	The element of music that relates to the controlled movement of music in time	Interval
9. *meter*	The aspect of rhythm concerned with regularly recurring groups of beats	Measure
10. *measure*	A metrical unit of time containing a primary accent	Melody
11. *Duple meter*	A meter containing two beats per measure	Meter
12. *Triple Meter*	A meter containing three beats per measure	Rhythm
13. *Syncopation*	The shifting of an accent from a strong to a weak beat	Syncopation
14. *Tempo*	The element of music that reflects the rate of speed of the beats	Tempo
15. *Dynamics*	The general term that refers to the degree of loudness and softness in music	Triple Meter

(General Review I continued on page 14.)

16. _Timbre_ — The distinctive tone quality of an instrument

17. _Pitch_ — The location of a tone in relation to high and low frequencies

18. _Score_ — The total complement of instrumental and/or vocal parts of a musical combination written out vertically in a combination of staves

19. _Orchestration_ — The art of setting music for instrumental combinations

20. _Suite_ — An instrumental work consisting of a number of movements related to a central idea

21. _Ostinato_ — A rhythmic or melodic pattern repeated persistently

22. _Cadenza_ — A solo passage within an orchestral work designed to display the virtuosity of the performer and the capacities of the instrument

23. _Form_ — The structural organization of a composition

24. _Ternary_ — A basic musical form planned on the principle of statement-departure-return

25. _Binary_ — A basic musical form comprised of two contrasting parts

26. _Style_ — The characteristic manner of presentation in any art

27. _Note_ — A symbol that denotes duration of musical sound

28. _Staff_ — The term for the arrangement of lines and spaces used for musical notation

29. _Clef_ — A symbol used to locate the pitches on a staff

30. _Rest_ — A symbol that denotes duration of silence

31. _Time Signature_ — A numerical symbol that specifies the meter

Binary
Cadenza
Clef
Form
Note
Orchestration
Ostinato
Pitch
Rest
Score
Staff
Style
Suite
Ternary
Timbre
Time Signature

1. Define melody

2. Define Harmony

3. Name and define the 3 componants of Time.

4. What kind of form has one theme and then alters it in some fashion several times?

5. What kind of form is Sonata - Allegro.

AURAL ANALYSIS

Tchaikovsky: NUTCRACKER SUITE

For each movement check (✔) the appropriate musical characteristics or events indicated in the Outline.

MINIATURE OVERTURE

1. Tempo: .... Cheerful, quick .... Quite slow

2. Tonal articulation: .... Staccato throughout .... Staccato vs. legato

3. Orchestration: .... Predominantly high pitched instruments

.... Predominantly low pitched instruments

One of the functions of an overture is to set the mood of the work it introduces. In a few words describe the atmosphere that prevails in this movement.

....

....

MARCH

1. The first part is characterized by repeated dialogue:

.... Brass answered by Strings .... Strings answered by Woodwinds

2. A short contrasting second part is also characterized by repeated dialogue:

.... Flutes and Clarinets answered by Violins and Violas

.... Violins and Violas answered by French Horns and Trumpets

3. Part three is a modified restatement of part one: .... Yes .... No

4. The three parts may be designated by: .... A B A .... A B C

5. The form of this movement is: .... Binary .... Ternary

DANCE OF THE SUGAR-PLUM FAIRY

1. After a pizzicato introduction, the featured instrument is the: .... Harp .... Celesta

2. The timbre of the featured instrument is counterposed by the timbres of the:

.... Bass Clarinet followed by Clarinet .... Bassoon followed by Oboe

3. When the orchestra stops and the featured instrument plays alone, this passage is called a:

.... Cadenza .... Cadence

RUSSIAN DANCE (TREPAK)

After listening to the entire movement, answer the following questions.

1. The basic tempo is: .... Molto vivace (Very lively) .... Adagio (Quite slow)

2. In the final portion of the movement there is an .... Accelerando .... Ritardando

ARAB DANCE

The movement begins with a repeated rhythmic figure played by the violas and cellos.

1. The next instrumental group heard is dominated by: .... Flutes .... Clarinets

2. The violins enter: .... Muted .... Unmuted

3. Two phrases (violins) are rounded off each time by a rhythmic figure played by:

   .... Triangle .... Tambourine

4. The next instrumental group heard is dominated by: .... French Horns .... Bassoons

5. In the ensuing portion of this movement three solo instruments are featured in turn:

   a) .... Oboe or .... Flute

   b) .... Clarinet or .... English Horn

   c) .... Bassoon or .... Clarinet

6. The repeated rhythmic figure that persists throughout the movement in the violas and cellos is called:

   .... Ostinato .... Cadenza

CHINESE DANCE

1. The most prominent instruments in the ostinato figure that opens the movement are:

   .... Bassoons .... Cellos

2. The melodic line is dominated by .... Violins and Violas .... Flute and Piccolo

DANCE OF THE TOY FLUTES

1. Part A of this movement is characterized by three flutes playing: .... Legato .... Staccato

2. The opening eight-bar phrase is repeated and then extended by a bridge-like passage that leads to

   .... Part B .... Restatement of Part A

3. Part B (a strongly contrasting section) opens with:

   .... Strings and Woodwinds .... Brass and Percussion

4. Part A is restated: .... Yes .... No

5. The form of this movement is: .... Binary .... Ternary

6. The meter of this movement is: .... Duple .... Triple

WALTZ OF THE FLOWERS

This movement consists of an introduction, a main section that is a compound form in which each part has its subdivisions, and a coda.

INTRODUCTION

1. Begins with woodwinds and horns answered by: .... Celesta .... Harp

2. Culminates in a cadenza featuring: .... Arpeggios .... Scale passages

MOVEMENT PROPER

PART A

3. Section *a* consists of two contrasting phrases in which

.... French Horns are answered by solo Clarinet

.... Woodwinds are answered by Strings

→ 4. *This is followed by a modified restatement of* a.

5. Section *b* consists of dialogue between

.... Strings and Woodwinds .... Brass and Strings

→ 6. *Section* b *is repeated.*

7. Section *a* is restated: .... Yes .... No

8. Section *b* is restated: .... Yes .... No

PART B

9. Section *c* has a new melody carried by

.... Flute and Oboe .... Trumpet and Trombone

→ 10. *Section* c *is repeated.*

11. Section *d* has a contrasting melody carried by

.... Brass .... Violas and Cellos

→ 12. *Section* d *is repeated.*

13. Section *c* (with a change in orchestration) is restated: .... Yes .... No

PART A

14. Part A is restated in modified form: .... Yes .... No

CODA

15. The Coda involves: .... Strings only; *pp* .... Full orchestra; ff

The meter of this movement is: .... Duple .... Triple

The form of this movement is: .... Compound Binary .... Compound Ternary

Notes

Part Two

NINETEENTH-CENTURY ROMANTICISM

Study Guide 7

CHAPTER 14

"Historians observe that style in art moves between two poles, the classic and the romantic."

GENERAL CHARACTERISTICS OF THE ROMANTIC MOVEMENT

Check (✔) those characteristics that are associated with romantic art of the nineteenth century.

1. .... The seeking of order, poise, serenity
2. ......✓...... The longing for strangeness, wonder, ecstacy
3. .... The objective viewpoint
4. ......✓...... Intense subjectivity, preoccupation with personal feelings
5. .... Need for moderation, desire for controlled emotion
6. ......✓...... A longing for the unknown
7. ......✓...... Individualism
8. ......✓...... Interest in simple folk and in children
9. ......✓...... Faith in man and in his destiny
10. .... Inspiration derived from the art of Ancient Greece
11. ......✓...... Intense awareness of nature
12. ......✓...... A leaning toward the fanciful and the picturesque
13. ......✓...... Intensely emotional type of expression
14. ......✓...... Exoticism
15. ......✓...... A fondness for the fantastic and the macabre
16. ......✓...... A multitude of color

MUSICAL CHARACTERISTICS OF THE ROMANTIC MOVEMENT

I. Check (✔) those characteristics associated with the music of the nineteenth century.

1. ....✓........ Improved instruments and better players, contributing to a new and more colorful kind of sound and expression

2. .... The church and palace as the chief centers of public musical activity

3. ....✓........ Increase in dynamic range; a tendency toward extremes and violent contrasts

4. .... Orchestra small in size

5. ....✓........ A preoccupation with the art of orchestration

6. ....✓........ Nationalism expressed in art music through the use of native folk songs and dances

7. ....✓........ Melody marked by lyricism

8. ....✓........ More colorful harmony through greater dissonance and chromaticism

9. ....✓........ Expansion of instrumental forms of the classical period

10. ....✓........ A tendency toward extreme emotional intensity

11. ....✓........ Tendency to infuse extramusical associations (elements outside the realm of sound) into music

II. Here are some expressive musical terms prevalent in romantic music. Supply the English equivalents.

espressivo _expressively_   con fuoco _with fire_   agitato _excited_

cantabile _song ful_   con amore _with love tenderly_ dolce _sweetly_

dolente _weeping sadly_   con passione _with fire with passion_   maestoso _majestic_

AURAL ANALYSIS
A Comparison of Styles: Classic vs. Romantic

I

Mozart: *THE IMPRESARIO — OVERTURE*

II

Wagner: *LOHENGRIN* — PRELUDE TO ACT III

Or others of your choice:

Composition ....   Composition ....

Composer ....   Composer ....

1. Check (✔) the attributes that are prominently displayed in each composition.

Melody:	.... Extended line(s) of a marked lyrical nature	.... Extended line(s) of a marked lyrical nature
	.... Moderately lyrical	.... Moderately lyrical
Dynamics:	.... Wide range; exploitation of extremes	.... Wide range; exploitation of extremes
	.... Moderate range predominates	.... Moderate range predominates
Pitch:	.... Wide range; exploitation of extremes	.... Wide range; exploitation of extremes
	.... Moderate range predominates	.... Moderate range predominates
Timbre:	.... Wide variety	.... Wide variety
	.... Moderate variety	.... Moderate variety
Orchestra:	.... Large size	.... Large size
	.... Moderate size	.... Moderate size
Sonority:	.... Tends toward a rich, colorful sound	.... Tends toward a rich, colorful sound
	.... Tends toward a light, sparse sound	.... Tends toward a light, sparse sound
Tempo:	.... Fluctuates conspicuously within a movement	.... Fluctuates conspicuously within a movement
	.... Fairly constant within a movement	.... Fairly constant within a movement
Expressive content:	.... Projected by the materials of music within a relatively moderate range	.... Projected by the materials of music within a relatively moderate range
	.... Projected by the materials of music within a relatively expanded range	.... Projected by the materials of music within a relatively expanded range

2. Composition I is representative of the .... period.

3. Composition II is representative of the .... period.

4. With respect to each period, list other stylistic attributes that may be present in each composition:

I. ....   II. ....

....

....

AURAL ANALYSIS
A Comparison of Styles: Classic vs. Romantic

<table>
<tr><td align="center">I</td><td align="center">II</td></tr>
</table>

Composition .... Composition ....

Composer .... Composer ....

1. Check (✔) the attributes that are prominently displayed in each composition.

Melody:	.... Extended line(s) of a marked lyrical nature	.... Extended line(s) of a marked lyrical nature
	.... Moderately lyrical	.... Moderately lyrical
Dynamics:	.... Wide range; exploitation of extremes	.... Wide range; exploitation of extremes
	.... Moderate range predominates	.... Moderate range predominates
Pitch:	.... Wide range; exploitation of extremes	.... Wide range; exploitation of extremes
	.... Moderate range predominates	.... Moderate range predominates
Timbre:	.... Wide variety	.... Wide variety
	.... Moderate variety	.... Moderate variety
Orchestra:	.... Large size	.... Large size
	.... Moderate size	.... Moderate size
Sonority:	.... Tends toward a rich, colorful sound	.... Tends toward a rich, colorful sound
	.... Tends toward a light, sparse sound	.... Tends toward a light, sparse sound
Tempo:	.... Fluctuates conspicuously within a movement	.... Fluctuates conspicuously within a movement
	.... Fairly constant within a movement	.... Fairly constant within a movement
Expressive content:	.... Projected by the materials of music within a relatively moderate range	.... Projected by the materials of music within a relatively moderate range
	.... Projected by the materials of music within a relatively expanded range	.... Projected by the materials of music within a relatively expanded range

2. Composition I is representative of the .... period.

3. Composition II is representative of the .... period.

4. With respect to each period, list other stylistic attributes that may be present in each composition:

I. .... II. ....

....

....

Study Guide 8

CHAPTER 16

1. The short lyric forms of nineteenth-century music are:

   a) .... b) ....

2. Refer to page 8 of the text. Find the following quotations and complete each with the author's words:

   a) "In the course of its wanderings it [the folk song] assumes a number of ...."

   [I.e. the identity of the original composer of the folk song is lost.]

   b) "Text and music (of the art song) are of known ...."

ART SONG

1. The three basic elements of an art song are:

   a) ....

   b) ....

   c) ....

2. The two main types of song structure are:

   a) ....

   b) ....

3. An intermediate type of song structure is a .... of ....

   and ....

4. The art song is often referred to by the German word ....

5. Two Germans whose lyric poetry inspired the art song composer were:

   a) .... b) ....

6. Some of the unique qualities of the art song are due to the versatile and expressive accompanying instrument, the

   ....

AURAL ANALYSIS
Art Song

Schumann: *Dichterliebe* — No. 1, *Im wunderschönen Monat Mai* (In the Wondrous Month of May)

German Text (Heinrich Heine: *Lyrisches Intermezzo*)

Free Translation

Im wunderschönen Monat Mai,	In the wondrous month of May,
Als alle Knospen sprangen,	When buds were everywhere unfolding,
Da ist in meinem Herzen	Here within my heart
Die Liebe aufgegangen.	Love came alive, awakened.
Im wunderschönen Monat Mai,	In the wondrous month of May,
Als alle Vögel sangen,	When all the birds were singing,
Da hab ich ihr gestanden	To her I now made known
Mein Sehnen und Verlangen.	My longing and my yearning.

Indicate the structure of this song. Check (✔).

.... Strophic .... Through-composed .... Combination

Mozart: *Das Veilchen* (The Violet), K. 476

German Text (Johann Wolfgang von Goethe)

Free Translation

Ein Veilchen auf der Wiese stand,	A violet stood in the field,
Gebückt in sich und unbekannt;	Bowed down, unknown and so forlorn;
Es war ein herzigs Veilchen.	It was a lovely violet.
Da kam eine junge Schäferin	Then came a youthful shepherdess
Mit leichtem Schritt und munterm Sinn	With tread so light and heart so gay
Daher, daher,	From far, from far,
Die Wiese her, und sang.	The meadow heard her song.
Ach! denkt das Veilchen, war ich nur	The violet thinks: "If I could be
Die schönste Blume der Natur,	The grandest flower of all outdoors,
Ach, nur ein kleines Weilchen,	For just a little while,
Bis mich das Liebchen abgepflückt	Until this girl has gathered me
Und an dem Busen matt gedrückt!	And to her bosom pressed me close!
Ach nur, ach nur	For just, for just,
Ein Viertelstündchen lang!	For just a quarter hour."
Ach! aber ach! das Mädchen kam	Alas, alas, the young girl came,
Und nicht in acht das Veilchen nahm,	Unmindful of the violet,
Ertrat das arme Veilchen.	She ground it underfoot.
Es sank und starb und freut' sich noch:	It sank, expired, and yet rejoiced:
Und sterb' ich denn, so sterb' ich doch	"If I'm to die, I die because
Durch sie, durch sie,	Of her, of her,
Zu ihren Füssen doch.	And gladly at her feet."
(Das arme Veilchen!	(Poor violet!
Es war ein herzigs Veilchen.)	It was a lovely violet.)

Indicate the structure of this song. Check (✔).

.... Strophic .... Through-composed .... Combination

Schubert: *Gretchen am Spinnrade* (Gretchen at the Spinning Wheel)

German Text (J. von Goethe: *Faust*)	*Free Translation*
Meine Ruh' ist hin, Mein Herz ist schwer, Ich finde, ich finde Sie nimmer und nimmer mehr.	My heart is heavy, my peace is gone, And I shall find it nevermore.
Wo ich ihn nicht hab', Ist mir das Grab, Die ganze Welt Ist mir vergällt.	When he is not beside me I could die; The whole world becomes hateful to me.
Mein armer Kopf Ist mir verrückt, Mein armer Sinn Ist mir zerstückt.	I feel as if I were out of my mind, I've lost all sanity.
Meine Ruh' ist hin, Mein Herz ist schwer, Ich finde, ich finde Sie nimmer und nimmer mehr.	My heart is heavy, my peace is gone, And I shall find it nevermore.
Nach ihm nur schau' ich Zum Fenster hinaus, Nach ihm nur geh' ich Aus dem Haus.	Him alone through the window I seek; For him alone I leave the house.
Sein hoher Gang, Sein' edle Gestalt, Seines Mundes Lächeln, Seiner Augen Gewalt,	His graceful bearing, his noble mien, His radiant smile, the power of his glance,
Und seiner Rede Zauberfluss, Sein Händedruck, Und ach, sein Kuss!	His bewitching speech, the clasp of his hand, And oh — his kiss!
Meine Ruh' ist hin, Mein Herz ist schwer, Ich finde, ich finde Sie nimmer und nimmer mehr.	My heart is heavy, my peace is gone, And I shall find it nevermore.
Mein Busen drängt Sich nach ihm hin. Ach, dürft ich fassen Und halten ihn!	With all my being I long for him, Ah, could I hold him in my arms!
Und küssen ihn, So wie ich wollt', An seinen Küssen Vergehen sollt',	And kiss him to my heart's desire, And on his kiss expire!
O könnt' ich ihn küssen, So wie ich wollt', An seinen Küssen Vergehen sollt',	Ah, could I kiss him to my heart's desire, And on his kiss expire!
Meine Ruh' ist hin, Mein Herz ist schwer!	My heart is heavy, my peace is gone!

(Questions on following page)

25

1. Indicate the structure of this song. Check (✔).

.... Strophic .... Through-composed .... Combination

2. What descriptive qualities are apparent in the piano accompaniment?

....

....

Other art songs of your choice:

1. Title .... Composer ....

.... Strophic .... Through-composed .... Combination

2. Title .... Composer ....

.... Strophic .... Through-composed .... Combination

3. Title .... Composer ....

.... Strophic .... Through-composed .... Combination

4. Title .... Composer ....

.... Strophic .... Through-composed .... Combination

5. Title .... Composer ....

.... Strophic .... Through-composed .... Combination

6. Title .... Composer ....

.... Strophic .... Through-composed .... Combination

Study Guide 9

CHAPTERS 16, 17, 18, 19

PIANO PIECE

Check (✔) the true statements:

1. ....✓.... Intimate personal expression and lyricism are qualities pre-eminently represented in the short lyric forms.

2. .... It was not until the twentieth century that the piano became a popular household instrument.

3. ....✓.... The nineteenth-century composer found the piano well-suited for the projection of romantic ideals.

4. ....✓.... In addition to short pieces with descriptive titles, nineteenth-century composers also cultivated the sonata and other types of music of a non-descriptive nature (pp. 72, 79, R87/S84f.).

5. ....✓.... The short piano piece as well as the art song became one of the most popular types of music in the romantic era.

6. ....✓.... The short lyric piano pieces are evidence of the romanticist's strong interest in the miniature in art.

AURAL ANALYSIS
Piano Piece

Schumann: Romance in F-Sharp, Opus 28, No. 2

1. Which of the following romantic qualities are present in this composition? Check (✔)

.... Lyricism   .... Wide pitch range   .... Descriptiveness

.... Emotional intensity   .... Wide dynamic range   .... Rich harmonic texture

                     .... Fluctuation in tempo

2. Is one consistent mood maintained throughout? Yes. ....   No. ....

Describe: ....

....

....

Chopin: Etude in E Major, Opus 10, No. 3

1. Which of the following romantic qualities are present in this composition? Check (✔)

.... Lyricism   .... Wide pitch range   .... Descriptiveness

.... Emotional intensity   .... Wide dynamic range   .... Rich harmonic texture

                                         .... Fluctuation in tempo

2. a) Describe the character of the opening section: ....

....

   b) Describe the character of the contrasting section: ....

....

   c) Does the opening idea return? .... Yes.   .... No.

3. Identify the form: ....

Liszt: *La Campanella* (The Little Bell)

1. Which of the following romantic qualities are present in this composition? Check (✔)

.... Lyricism   .... Descriptiveness   .... Wide pitch range

.... Emotional intensity   .... Fluctuation in tempo   .... Rich harmonic texture

                                         .... Wide dynamic range

2. Indicate how the music reflects the title: ....

....

Other piano pieces of your choice

Title ....   Composer ....

1. Which of the following romantic qualities are present in this composition? Check (✔)

.... Lyricism   .... Descriptiveness   .... Wide pitch range

.... Emotional intensity   .... Fluctuation in tempo   .... Rich harmonic texture

                                         .... Wide dynamic range

2. Is one consistent mood maintained throughout? .... Yes.   .... No.

   Describe: ....

....

3. Identify the form: ....

Title ....   Composer ....

1. Which of the following romantic qualities are present in this composition? Check (✔)

.... Lyricism   .... Descriptiveness   .... Wide pitch range

.... Emotional intensity   .... Fluctuation in tempo   .... Rich harmonic texture

                                         .... Wide dynamic range

2. Is one consistent mood maintained throughout? .... Yes.   .... No.

   Describe: ....

....

3. Identify the form: ....

Study Guide 10

CHAPTER R22/S20

1. Instrumental music that has a literary or pictorial association supplied by the composer is called ....*program* ....*music* ....

2. Instrumental music devoid of literary or pictorial connotations is called ...*absolute*........*music*...

3. List four varieties of program music with the title and composer of a musical composition representative of each type.

TYPE	TITLE	COMPOSER
a) *Concert Overture*	*see p. 88*	
b) *Incidental Music*	"	
c) *Program Symphony*	"	
d) *Symphonic Poem*	"	

4. Underline the word or phrase in parentheses that accurately completes the statement.

   a) The distinctive characteristics of a *concert overture* are:

   It is a (single-) (multi-) movement work.

   It (is) (is not) associated with an opera.

   It (is) (is not) usually structured in sonata-allegro form.

   b) The distinctive characteristics of *incidental music* are:

   It is a (single-) (multi-) movement work.

   It (was) (was not) conceived as an adjunct to a play.

   c) The distinctive characteristics of the *program symphony* are:

   Its basic structure (is) (it not) derived from the classical symphony.

   It (does) (does not) retain the character of a symphony in conjunction with programmatic associations.

   d) The symphonic poem originated with (Franz Schubert) (Franz Liszt).

   e) The distinctive characteristics of the *symphonic poem* are:

   It is a (single-) (multi-) movement work for orchestra.

   Its free form (is) (is not) conditioned by the contents of its literary or pictorial association.

LISTENING GUIDE

Tchaikovsky: OVERTURE-FANTASY: *ROMEO AND JULIET* (1869)

Key: B minor

Meter: **C** ($\frac{4}{4}$)

Instrumentation: Piccolo, 2 Flutes, 2 Oboes, 2 Clarinets, English Horn, 2 Bassoons, 4 Horns, 2 Trumpets, 3 Trombones, Tuba, 3 Timpani, Cymbals, Bass Drum, Harp, Violins, Violas, Cellos, Double Basses.

Introduction (Friar Laurence)

Tempo: Andante non tanto
      quasi Moderato

1. Chorale: clarinets and bassoons, *p*, evoke an organ-like quality.

2. Strings and horn create foreboding atmosphere. Section ends with harp arpeggios.
3. Strings pizzicato accompany woodwind chorale.
4. Item 2 restated; modified orchestration.
5. Intensification of mood: cresc., accel., rise in pitch; persistent timpani roll, strings, woodwinds, brasses.
6. Short transition (strings vs. woodwinds) builds to

Movement Proper

Tempo: Allegro giusto

Form: Sonata-allegro

EXPOSITION

First theme group (Feud)

7. Brusque rhythmic figure; tutti, *f*.

8. Strings vs. woodwinds in imitation — first theme motivic fragment.
9. Expansion: running scale passage, strings, punctuated by syncopated chords — cresc. to *ff*.
10. Bridge (first theme motivic fragment: flute, clarinet, bassoon, cellos and basses) leads to

30

Second theme group (Love)   11. *a*) English horn and muted violas (marked lyricism).

                                   b) Muted strings (repetitions and sequences).

        12. Second theme *a* expanded.

Codetta   13. Closing section, *pp* (persistent harp accompaniment).

DEVELOPMENT   14. This section is dominated by motives of first theme (feud) and introductory chorale (Friar Laurence).

        15. Running scale passage in strings punctuated by syncopated chords, *ff*, leads to

RECAPITULATION

First theme group   16. First theme (feud), tutti, *ff*.

Second theme group   17. Second theme (love) opens with *b* followed by expanded version of *a*.

        18. First theme and chorale melody again prominently displayed.

        19. Recapitulation ends with timpani roll, *ff* ⟩ *p*.

Epilogue   20. Ostinato timpani figure accompanies second theme fragment.

        21. Chorale: woodwinds and horns.

        22. Harp introduces return of second theme in strings.

        23. Conclusion: timpani roll and syncopated chords — tutti, *ff*.

After listening to the

Overture-Fantasy: *Romeo and Juliet*,

complete the Program Music Analysis Outline, p. 32.

PROGRAM MUSIC ANALYSIS

Composition .... Composer ....

1. Check (✔) the statements that apply to this composition:

.... Concert Overture   .... Single-movement work

.... Incidental Music   .... Multi-movement work

.... Program Symphony   .... Sonata-allegro form

.... Symphonic Poem   .... Free form

.... Associated with an opera   .... Cyclical structure

.... An integral part of the original play

2. Check (✔) the stylistic characteristics prominently displayed:

Melody: .... Extended line(s) of a marked lyrical nature

                        .... Absence of lyricism

Dynamics: .... Wide range; exploitation of extremes

                        .... Moderate range predominates

Pitch: .... Wide range; exploitation of extremes

                        .... Narrow range

Timbre: .... Wide variety

                        .... Limited variety

Sonority: .... Tends toward a rich, colorful sound

                        .... Tends toward a light, sparse sound

Tempo: .... A variety of tempos

                        .... One tempo throughout

Expressive content: .... Projected by the materials of music within a relatively moderate range

                        .... Projected by the materials of music within a relatively expanded range

3. This composition is representative of the .... period.

4. With respect to this period, list other stylistic attributes that may be present in this composition:

....

....

....

....

....

....

PROGRAM MUSIC ANALYSIS

Composition .... Composer ....

1. Check (✔) the statements that apply to this composition:

.... Concert Overture   .... Single-movement work

.... Incidental Music   .... Multi-movement work

.... Program Symphony   .... Sonata-allegro form

.... Symphonic Poem   .... Free form

.... Associated with an opera   .... Cyclical structure

.... An integral part of the original play

2. Check (✔) the stylistic characteristics prominently displayed:

Melody: .... Extended line(s) of a marked lyrical nature

.... Absence of lyricism

Dynamics: .... Wide range; exploitation of extremes

.... Moderate range predominates

Pitch: .... Wide range; exploitation of extremes

.... Narrow range

Timbre: .... Wide variety

.... Limited variety

Sonority: .... Tends toward a rich, colorful sound

.... Tends toward a light, sparse sound

Tempo: .... A variety of tempos

.... One tempo throughout

Expressive content: .... Projected by the materials of music within a relatively moderate range

.... Projected by the materials of music within a relatively expanded range

3. This composition is representative of the .... period.

4. With respect to this period, list other stylistic attributes that may be present in this composition:

....

....

....

....

....

....

33

PROGRAM MUSIC ANALYSIS

Composition .... Composer ....

1. Check (✔) the statements that apply to this composition:

.... Concert Overture   .... Single-movement work

.... Incidental Music   .... Multi-movement work

.... Program Symphony   .... Sonata-allegro form

.... Symphonic Poem   .... Free form

.... Associated with an opera   .... Cyclical structure

.... An integral part of the original play

2. Check (✔) the stylistic characteristics prominently displayed:

Melody: .... Extended line(s) of a marked lyrical nature

         .... Absence of lyricism

Dynamics: .... Wide range; exploitation of extremes

         .... Moderate range predominates

Pitch: .... Wide range; exploitation of extremes

         .... Narrow range

Timbre: .... Wide variety

         .... Limited variety

Sonority: .... Tends toward a rich, colorful sound

         .... Tends toward a light, sparse sound

Tempo: .... A variety of tempos

         .... One tempo throughout

Expressive content: .... Projected by the materials of music within a relatively moderate range

         .... Projected by the materials of music within a relatively expanded range

3. This composition is representative of the .... period.

4. With respect to this period, list other stylistic attributes that may be present in this composition:

....

....

....

....

....

....

Study Guide 11

CHAPTER R28/S25

1. Political and sociological conditions in nineteenth-century Europe encouraged the growth of musical ....
   ....*nationalism*........................... .

2. List four ways in which the surge of nationalism finds expression in music:
   ....*songs & dances of the people*........   *national heros/beauty of the country*
   .....*folklore or sagas of*...................   *historic events*....................

3. List six composers, identify their nationalities, and for each one name a composition that exemplifies musical nationalism:

COMPOSER	NATIONALITY	COMPOSITION
see p. 111		

4. Nationalism was inspired by a strong identification with native culture. The tendency to seek out qualities of a foreign culture and distant locale is called ....*exoticism*........................ .

5. List six composers, identify their nationalities, and for each one name a composition that exemplifies musical exoticism:

COMPOSER	NATIONALITY	COMPOSITION
see p. 112, 113.		

NATIONALISM — EXOTICISM ANALYSIS

Composition .... Composer ....

1. Check (✔) the statements that apply to this composition:

.... Concert Overture   .... Inspired by native culture

.... Incidental Music   .... Inspired by foreign culture

.... Program Symphony   .... Native folk idiom

.... Symphonic Poem   .... Foreign folk idiom

This composition exemplifies .... Nationalism .... Exoticism

2. Check (✔) the stylistic characteristics prominently displayed:

Melody: .... Extended line(s) of a marked lyrical nature

       .... Absence of lyricism

Dynamics: .... Wide range; exploitation of extremes

       .... Moderate range predominates

Pitch: .... Wide range; exploitation of extremes

       .... Narrow range

Timbre: .... Wide variety

       .... Limited variety

Sonority: .... Tends toward a rich, colorful sound

       .... Tends toward a light, sparse sound

Tempo: .... A variety of tempos

       .... One tempo throughout

Expressive content: .... Projected by the materials of music within a relatively moderate range

       .... Projected by the materials of music within a relatively expanded range

3. This composition is representative of the .... period.

4. With respect to this period, list other stylistic attributes that may be present in this composition:

....

....

....

Study Guide 12

CHAPTER R30/S26

1. Match each of the following items to its appropriate association:

Absolute music	Development	Recapitulation	Theme
Bridge (Transition)	Exposition	Scherzo	Trio
Coda	Motive	Sonata-allegro	
Codetta	Movement	Symphony	

a) .... The term used to designate non-programmatic music

b) .... An orchestral work in several contrasting movements with the first and possibly other movements in sonata-allegro form

c) .... A complete and comparatively independent part of a musical work

d) .... A musical form comprised of three distinct, integrated sections referred to as Exposition, Development, Recapitulation

e) .... A distinctive musical idea which serves as a building block or germinating element in a musical work

f) .... A constituent fragment of a theme

g) .... The structural division in sonata-allegro form during which the thematic groups are initially presented

h) .... A passage connecting two contrasting ideas or keys

i) .... The closing section in the Exposition

j) .... The structural division in sonata-allegro form marked by increased tension, in which the material of the Exposition is explored and exploited

k) .... The structural division in sonata-allegro form during which the themes of the Exposition are restated in modified form

l) .... The concluding section of a movement

m) .... Music of a whimsical, rhythmic, often humorous nature — frequently the third movement of a nineteenth-century symphony

n) .... The middle section of the scherzo

2. Outline sonata-allegro form by arranging the following structural components in proper sequence:

Coda   Development   First-theme group   Second-theme group
Codetta   Exposition   Recapitulation

a) ....

   ....

   ....

   ....

b) ....

c) ....

   ....

   ....

   ....

CHAPTERS R32/S27, R36/S30

Match each item in Column II to its appropriate association in Column I:

COLUMN I		COLUMN II
1.	Restatement of a musical pattern at a higher or lower pitch	Cadenza (p. R162/S135)
2.	The recurrence in later movements of themes from earlier movements	Concerto (p. R161/S134)
3.	An extensive work for one or more solo instruments and orchestra	Cyclical Structure (p. R147/S123)
4.	An Italian word that refers to the orchestra as a whole	Sequence (p. R145/S120)
5.	A solo passage in the manner of an improvisation interpolated into a concerto	Tutti (p. R162/S135)

LISTENING GUIDE

Dvořák: SYMPHONY NO. 9 in E Minor, Opus 95 — *From the New World* (1893)

Movement: First

Key: E minor

Instrumentation: 2 Flutes, 2 Oboes, 2 Clarinets, 2 Bassoons, 4 Horns, 2 Trumpets, 3 Trombones, 3 Timpani, Violins, Violas, Cellos, Double Basses.

Introduction

Tempo: Adagio

Meter: $\frac{4}{8}$

1. a) Serene melody: low strings, *pp*

   b) Echo: woodwinds, *p*

2. a) *ff* outbursts: strings — timpani — winds

   b) *pp*, cellos and basses

3. a) Arpeggio figure: strings and horns

   b) Timpani *ff* ⟩ *p*

Movement Proper

Tempo: Allegro molto

Meter: $\frac{2}{4}$

EXPOSITION

First theme group

4. {a) Arpeggio figure: horns
   {b) Dotted figure, staccato: clarinets and bassoons

5. a) Expansion: first theme group

   b) Bridge to

Second theme group | 6. a) Folk-like tune: flute and oboe, *p*; restated by violins

b) Expansion, involving sequences

c) Bridge to

Third theme group

(Codetta) | 7. a) "Char-i-ot": solo flute, *p*

(Char - i - ot___)

b) Final cadence: tutti, *ff*

Exposition may be repeated

DEVELOPMENT | 8. Third and first themes explored and exploited in alternation

9. Transition: first theme motive; sequences; *pp* ◀── *f*

RECAPITULATION | Exposition substantially restated

First theme group | 10. {a) Arpeggio figure: horns
{b) Dotted figure, staccato: clarinets and bassoons

11. Transition to

Second theme group | 12. a) Folk-like tune: solo flute, *p*

b) Expansion involving sequences

c) Bridge to

Third theme group | 13. a) "Char-i-ot": solo flute, *p*

b) "Char-i-ot": horns, *f*, leads to

Coda | 14. Dominated by first theme, tutti, *ff*

After listening to this movement, complete the

Absolute Music Analysis Outline

(*Eighteenth-Nineteenth Centuries*), p. 41.

ABSOLUTE MUSIC ANALYSIS
Eighteenth-Nineteenth Centuries

Composition .....Symphony....#4.......................... Composer .....Brahms.........................

1. Identify the compositional type (such as sonata, <u>symphony</u>, concerto, suite, fugue, etc.): ....

2. Indicate the number of movements and the structural design of each movement considered. Number of move-

   ments: .....4...

FORM

1st movement: .....Sonata....Alleg......   4th movement: .....Theme & Var.............

2nd movement: .....A BA......................   5th movement: ....

3rd movement: .....A BA......................   6th movement: ....

3. Check (✔) the attributes that are prominently displayed in this movement:

   Melody: ......✔...... Extended line(s) of a marked lyrical nature

                                  .... Moderately lyrical

   Dynamics: ......✔...... Wide range; exploitation of extremes

                                  .... Moderate range predominates

   Pitch: ......✔...... Wide range; exploitation of extremes

                                  .... Moderate range predominates

   Timbre: ......✔...... Wide variety

                                  .... Moderate variety

   Sonority: ......✔...... Tends toward a rich, colorful sound

                                  .... Tends toward a light, sparse sound

   Tempo: ......✔...... Fluctuates conspicuously within a movement

                                  .... Fairly constant within a movement

   Expressive content: .... Projected by the materials of music within a relatively moderate range

                                  ......✔...... Projected by the materials of music within a relatively expanded range

4. This composition is representative of the .....Romantic................. period.

5. With respect to this period, list other stylistic attributes that may be present in this composition.

   ....

   ....

   ....

LISTENING GUIDE

Mendelssohn: VIOLIN CONCERTO IN E MINOR, Opus 64 (1844)

Movement:	First
Key:	E minor
Tempo:	Allegro molto appassionato
Meter:	$\mathbf{C}$ ($\frac{2}{2}$)
Form:	Sonata-allegro
Instrumentation:	2 Flutes, 2 Oboes, 2 Clarinets, 2 Bassoons, 2 Horns, 2 Trumpets, 2 Timpani, Solo Violin, Violins, Violas, Cellos, Double Basses.

EXPOSITION

First theme group

1. Extended lyrical line: solo violin, high register

2. Expansion: triplet figure prominent in solo violin
3. First theme restated: orchestral tutti, *ff*
4. Transition — new melodic line: orchestra imitated by solo violin; expansion involving solo display passages

Second theme group

5. Melody presented by flutes and clarinets over solo violin *pedal point*

6. Second theme restated and extended: solo violin

Codetta

7. Closing section based on first theme; triplet figure again prominent
8. Tutti, *ff*, first theme motive; sequential figures solo violin, *dim.* bridges to

DEVELOPMENT

9. Exploration of transitional idea and first theme
10. a) Descending sequences: solo violin
    b) Tutti (first theme motive) *pp* ——— *ff*

CADENZA

11. Virtuosic display involving:

    arpeggios

    wide pitch range

    trills

    chords

    thematic fragment

12. Final arpeggio passage becomes accompaniment figure to

RECAPITULATION

First theme group   13. First theme, tutti, *pp*

14. Transition theme: a) tutti, *ff*

                    b) solo violin

Second theme group   15. Second theme: a) woodwinds

                    b) solo violin

Coda   16. Codetta material restated

17. Tutti, *ff*, first theme motive; solo violin, sequential figures; *dim.* bridges to

18. Più presto (faster) concluding section.

After listening to this movement, complete the
Absolute Music Analysis Outline
(*Eighteenth-Nineteenth Centuries*), p. 44.

ABSOLUTE MUSIC ANALYSIS
Eighteenth-Nineteenth Centuries

Composition .... Composer ....

1. Identify the compositional type (such as sonata, symphony, concerto, suite, fugue, etc.): ....

2. Indicate the number of movements and the structural design of each movement considered. Number of movements: ....

FORM

1st movement: .... 4th movement: ....

2nd movement: .... 5th movement: ....

3rd movement: .... 6th movement: ....

3. Check (✔) the attributes that are prominently displayed in this movement:

Melody: .... Extended line(s) of a marked lyrical nature
                   .... Moderately lyrical

Dynamics: .... Wide range; exploitation of extremes
                   .... Moderate range predominates

Pitch: .... Wide range; exploitation of extremes
                   .... Moderate range predominates

Timbre: .... Wide variety
                   .... Moderate variety

Sonority: .... Tends toward a rich, colorful sound
                   .... Tends toward a light, sparse sound

Tempo: .... Fluctuates conspicuously within a movement
                   .... Fairly constant within a movement

Expressive content: .... Projected by the materials of music within a relatively moderate range
                   .... Projected by the materials of music within a relatively expanded range

4. This composition is representative of the .... period.

5. With respect to this period, list other stylistic attributes that may be present in this composition.

....

....

....

Study Guide 13

CHAPTER R39/S32

1. Match each item in the following list to its appropriate association with respect to opera:

Aria	Ballet	Chorus	Ensemble
Libretto	Opera	Orchestra	Recitative

a) *Opera*   A drama that is sung

b) *Recitative*   A type of musical declamation that follows the natural inflections of speech

c) *Aria*   A solo song — a lyric moment in the action

d) *Ensemble*   A small vocal group consisting of three or more voices

e) *Chorus*   The large or mass vocal group

f) *Orchestra*   The instrumental accompanying body which also functions independently in the overture, interludes, etc.

g) *Ballet*   A component that provides the diversion of the dance

h) *Libretto*   The text

2. Check (✔) the true statements:

a) ...X... Opera as a musical poetic drama often transcends the logic of reality.

b) .... The aria is less melodious than the recitative.

c) .... There are no musical plays with spoken dialogue.

d) ...X... An operatic ensemble number may involve several characters simultaneously projecting a variety of contrasting emotions.

CHAPTERS R41/S34, R44/S35

1. The term Wagner used to describe his type of opera is *Opera — drama*. (p. R185/S152)

2. The Wagnerian treatment of melody that supplanted the recitative and aria in his operas is called *endless melody* (p. R186/S153)

3. Basic themes that recur throughout a Wagnerian opera and are associated with a character or idea are called *liet-motif* (p. R186/S154)

4. The Italian term associated with the movement toward realism in late nineteenth-century opera is *verismo* (p. R207/S164)

LISTENING GUIDE
Operatic Components

Puccini: LA BOHÈME — Scenes

ACT I — from Mimi's entrance to the end of Rodolfo's aria

Setting: The garret room of the Bohemians. Rodolfo is alone, trying to work. Mimi, a neighbor, stops by.

COMPONENT	ITALIAN TEXT	ENGLISH SUMMARY
RECITATIVE	*Rodolfo:* Non sono in vena. *(A timid knock at the door.)* Chi è là? *Mimi:* Scusi. *Rodolfo:* Una donna! . . .	Rodolfo is not in the mood for work. Mimi enters; her candle has gone out. She has a fit of coughing, and Rodolfo offers her some wine. She lights her candle and prepares to leave, then realizes she has misplaced her key. A gust of winds blows out both their candles, and they begin to look for the key on the floor, in the dark. Rodolfo finds it, but slips it into his pocket and pretends to search further. Their hands touch in the dark.
ARIA	*Rodolfo:* Che gelida manina, Se la lasci riscalder. Cercar che giova? Al buio non si trova. . . .	"How cold your little fingers . . . Let me warm them here in mine." Rodolfo describes his life as a poet, and tells Mimi that her eyes surpass in enchantment his poetic dreams. He asks her to tell him who she is.
ARIA	*Mimi:* Mi chiamano Mimì, Ma il mio nome è Lucia. . . .	"I'm known as Mimi, But my real name is Lucia." She is a seamstress who lives alone, and likes to make imitation flowers — but, alas, they have no fragrance.
RECITATIVE	*Schaunard:* Eh! Rodolfo! *Colline:* Rodolfo! *Marcello:* Olà! Non senti?	Rodolfo's friends call up from the courtyard, urging him to hurry. He tells them he is not alone; they should go ahead to the restaurant and reserve a table.
DUET	*Rodolfo:* O soave fanciulla, o dolce viso Di mite circonfuso alba lunar, In te, ravviso il sogno . . .	"O adorable vision! Maiden enveloped in the splendor of the moon!" Rodolfo is enchanted by Mimi's beauty, and, as they go off arm in arm to the café, they declare their mutual love.

ACT II — Opening Scene

Setting: Outside the Café Momus in the Latin Quarter. A crowd of townspeople, soldiers, children, and vendors is milling around.

COMPONENT	ITALIAN TEXT	ENGLISH SUMMARY
CHORUS	*Vendors:* Aranci, datteri! Caldi i marroni! *The Crowd:* Ah! quanta folla! Che chiasso!	The vendors hawk their wares, echoed by street urchins, while the crowd exclaims on the lively scene. (Eventually Rodolfo and Mimi arrive to join their companions.

ACT III — Farewell Scene

 Setting: Outside a tavern where Marcello and Musetta are working. It is winter. Mimi has told Rodolfo that she must leave him.

DUET

Rodolfo: Dunque è proprio finita.
 Te ne vai, la mia piccina?!
 Addio sogni d'amor! . . .

"Then everything is finished. You are leaving, my little one". They recall together the joys and sorrows of love. From inside the tavern is heard the sound of plates and glasses being broken. Marcello and Musetta come running out.

ENSEMBLE
(Quartet)

Marcello: Che facevi? Che dicevi,
Musetta: Che vuoi dir?
Marcello: — Presso il foco a quel signore?

"You were flirting with that gentleman!" "What do you mean?" After a violent argument (during which Rodolfo and Mimi continue their duet), Musetta and Marcello part in anger.

DUET

Mimi: Sempre tua per la vita,
Rodolfo: Ci lasceremo
Mimi: Ci lasceremo alla stagion dei
 fior . . .

The curtain falls on Rodolfo and Mimi in a mood of nostalgia.

OPERA ANALYSIS
Nineteenth Century

Opera .... Composer ....

1. Check (✔) the components present in this opera:

.... Overture or Opening Prelude   .... Recitative

.... Other Prelude(s)   .... Aria

.... Entr'acte Music   .... Ensemble(s)

.... Orchestra Interlude(s)   .... Chorus

.... Ballet   .... Spoken Dialogue

2. List the principal characters in this opera and their voice ranges (Soprano, Alto, Tenor, Bass):

....

....

....

....

3. With respect to the romantic period, list stylistic characteristics present in this opera:

....

....

....

....

....

....

....

General Review II.   Nineteenth-Century Romanticism

Match each item in the following list to its appropriate association:

Absolute Music	Lied	Piano	Through-composed
Concert Overture	Lyricism	Program Music	Timbre
Dynamics	Orchestra	Public Concert Hall	
Harmony	Orchestration	Strophic	

1. *Timbre*   An element of music through which a great variety of tone color is achieved

2. *Public Concert Hall*   Replaced the aristocratic palace and church as the chief center of musical activity

3. *Dynamics*   An element of music in which the extremes of tonal volume are exploited

4. *Orchestra*   The performance medium whose enlarged proportions result in richer sonorities

5. *Orchestration*   The part of the compositional process dealing with the complex combination of instrumental timbres

6. *lyricism*   A songlike quality found in instrumental music that seeks to emulate the essence of vocal melody

7. *Harmony*   An element of music in which expanded dissonance and chromaticism are manifested

8. *Lied*   The German word for art song

9. *Strophic*   A type of song structure in which all the stanzas are set to the same music

10. *Through-composed*   A type of song structure in which the music varies with each stanza of the text

11. *piano*   The keyboard instrument of greatest popularity in this era

12. *Program Music*   A designation for instrumental music with literary or pictorial associations supplied by the composer

13. *Absolute Music*   Instrumental music for which the composer has not indicated any non-musical association.

14. *Concert Overture*   A type of program music usually in sonata-allegro form deriving its inspiration from a dramatic source but related to the theater in title only

(General Review II continued on page 50.)

Match each item in the following list to its appropriate association:

Aria	Exoticism	Nationalism	Sonata-allegro
Concerto	Incidental Music	Opera	Symphonic Poem
Cyclical Structure	Leitmotifs	Program Symphony	Symphony
Endless Melody	Music Drama	Recitative	Verismo

1. _Incidental Music_   Music intended to complement the performance of a play

2. _Program Sym_   A multi-movement composition, cast in the general form of a symphony but programmatic in content

3. _Symphonic poem_   A single-movement programmatic type of orchestral piece introduced by Liszt

4. _Nationalism_   The impulse to compose music inspired by elements native to the composer's culture

5. _Exoticism_   The impulse to compose music inspired by elements foreign to the composer's culture.

6. _Symphony_   An orchestral work in several contrasting movements, with the first and possibly other movements in sonata-allegro form

7. _Sonata Allegro_   A structural design expanded, extended, and treated flexibly in the romantic era

8. _Cyclical Structure_   A procedure in composition that involves the use of the same thematic material in several movements of a multi-movement work

9. _Concerto_   An extensive work for one or more solo instruments and orchestra

10. _Opera_   A drama that is sung

11. _Recitative_   In opera, a type of musical declamation following the natural inflections of speech

12. _Aria_   In opera, a solo lyric song

13. _Music Drama_   Wagner's term for his kind of opera

14. _Endless Melody_   Wagner's type of melodic treatment, which supplanted the recitative and aria in his operas

15. _Leitmotifs_   Basic themes that recur throughout a Wagnerian opera

16. _Verismo_   A trend in Italian opera of the late romantic period that displayed a preference for themes drawn from everyday life

Part Three

MORE MATERIALS OF MUSIC

Study Guide 14

Review the material in Chapters 3, 4, and 13.

CHAPTER R45/S36

Complete the following statements:

1. The central tone around which a family of tones revolve and to which they ultimately gravitate may be designated in three ways:

   a) .... b) .... c) ....

2. A group of related tones (no order implied) with a common center or Tonic is called a ....

3. The sense of relatedness to a central tone is known as ....

4. The distance, and the relationship, between two tones is called an ....

5. The distance from one tone to the next tone of the same name (above or below) is called an ....

6. In Western music, the octave is divided into .... equal intervals.

7. In our musical system, the smallest intervallic unit is a ....

8. The interval encompasing two adjacent semitones is a ....

9. A series of tones arranged in consecutive order, ascending or descending, is a ....

10. The twelve semitones of the octave, arranged in consecutive order, constitute a .... scale.

11. The music of the classic and romantic periods is based on two contrasting scales: ....
    and ....

12. The intervallic relationship between the first and last tones of the major and minor scales is an ....

13. The following pattern represents the formula for the .... scale:

	whole step		whole step		half step		whole step		whole step		whole step		half step	
1		2		3		4		5		6		7		8
Do		Re		Mi		Fa		Sol		La		Ti		Do

14. Because of cultural conditioning, we have come to respond to certain tones of the scale in terms of
    .... and ....

15. The quality of rest or activity attributed to any tone is determined not by its intrinsic nature but by its position in the ....

16. The pattern of whole and half steps of a scale determines the ....

17. The minor mode differs from the major primarily in that its .... degree is lowered a half step.

CHAPTER R46/S37

I. Underline the correct completions:

1. The act of shifting all the tones of a composition a uniform distance to a higher or lower level of pitch is called:

   Modulation   Transposition   Orchestration   Chromaticism

2. When a piece of music is transposed it is shifted to another:

   Mode   Tempo   Key   Meter

3. The process of passing from one key to another is known as:

   Modulation   Chromaticism   Scale   Tonality

4. The twelve-tone scale that includes all the semitones of the octave is called:

   Diatonic   Chromatic

5. The major and minor scales are called:

   Diatonic   Chromatic

6. The home key serves the purpose of:

   Unity   Variety

7. Contrasting keys contribute to:

   Unity   Variety

II. Check (✔) the true statements:

1. .... When a piece is transposed, the level of pitch is changed but the melody line remains the same.

2. .... Modulation tends to create a heightened sense of activity.

3. .... Nineteenth-century romantic music does not contain frequent modulations.

4. .... A key is sustained by the tones directly related to its tonic, whereas the prominence of chromatic tones tends to weaken the key.

5. .... Harmonies derived from tones extraneous to a key are known as *chromatic.*

6. .... Harmonies based on the tones of the major and minor keys are known as *diatonic.*

7. .... Music of the late eighteenth century (classical period) is predominantly diatonic.

8. .... Music of the nineteenth century (romantic period) shows a tendency towards chromatic harmony.

9. .... The interrelationship between home and contrasting keys plays a part in the structural design of a composition.

10. .... The eighteenth-century sonata developed without regard to key relationships.

NAME ....   CLASS ....   DATE ....

Study Guide 15

Review the material in Chapter R30/S26

(handwritten: Themes, Sonata form)

CHAPTERS R47/S38, R48/S39

Complete the following:

1. The basic idea in the construction of a musical work is called a ..... *theme* ..... or ..... *subject* ......

2. Unfolding a theme's latent energies and exploiting its capacity for growth is known as ..... *develop* .....

3. The process of thematic development involves a variety of procedures such as:
   a) *repetition* — exact or varied reiteration (p. R224/S178)
   b) *sequence* — the restatement of an idea at a higher or lower pitch level (p. R224/S178)
   c) *(harmony) modulation* — frequent changes of key (p. R224/S178)
   d) *inversion* — a musical idea turned upside down (p. R226/S180)
   e) *augmentation* — the expansion of original note values into longer ones (p. R226/S180)
   f) *diminution* — the contraction of original note values into shorter ones (p. R226/S180)

4. In the process of development, the original idea (theme) may also be varied in regard to:
   a) *melody*   b) *rhythm*   c) *dynamics*
   d) *harmony*   e) *timbre*   f) *register*

5. The smallest fragment of a theme that forms a melodic-rhythmic unit is called a ..... *motif* .....

6. In the broadest sense, the term ..... *sonata* ..... indicates a piece of instrumental music; the term ..... *cantata* ....., a piece of vocal music.

7. The sonata cycle written for
   one or two instruments is called ..... *sonata* .....
   three instruments is called ..... *trio* .....
   four instruments is called ..... *quartet* .....
   five instruments is called ..... *quintet* .....
   orchestra is called ..... *symphony* .....
   solo instrument and orchestra is called ..... *concerto* .....

8. The three terms used in referring to the structure of the first movement of a sonata are:
   ..... *sonata-allegro* ..... form.
   ..... *sonata* ..... form.
   ..... *first-movement* ..... form.

53

9. The principle of Statement-Departure-Return is the foundation of ......*sonata - allegro*...... form.

10. Sonata-allegro form has three sections, which are called

   a) ......*exposition*......   b) ......*development*......   c) ......*recapitulation*......

11. In the Exposition, the distinctive musical idea (and its expansion) that establishes the home key is called the ......*first*...... theme group.

× 12. A passage that leads to a contrasting section is called a ......*bridge*...... or ......*transition*.......

13. In the Exposition, the distinctive musical idea (and its expansion) that establishes the ......*contrasting*...... key is called the second theme group.

14. The section that closes the Exposition in the contrasting key is called ......*codetta*.......

× 15. In the ......*development*...... section, frequent modulations contribute to the increase of tension.

16. The Recapitulation is a modified restatement of the ......*exposition*.......

17. The final portion, which completes a movement, is called ......*recapitulation*.......

18. Check (✔) the traditional key areas in sonata-allegro form:

		HOME KEY	CONTRASTING KEYS
Exposition	Theme Group 1	×	
	Theme Group 2		×
	Codetta		×
Development			×
Recapitulation	Theme Group 1	×	
	Theme Group 2	×	
	Coda	×	

CHAPTERS R48/S39, R49/S40

I. Match each form in the following list to its appropriate association:

A Minuet   C Rondo   D Rondo-Sonata

B Scherzo   E Theme and Variations

1. *E Theme & Variations*   A musical structure in which a theme is stated and then presented in a series of modifications.

2. *A Minuet*   A composition in triple meter, of dance origin, frequently serving as the third movement of the sonata cycle

3. *B Scherzo*   A composition that replaced the minuet as a movement of the nineteenth-century symphony

4. *C Rondo*   A form characterized by the recurrence of a principal theme group in alternation with contrasting sections

5. *D Rondo-Sonata*   A design that combines the spirit of the rondo with the structural characteristics of sonata-allegro form

II. Check (✔) the true statements:

1. .... Sonata-allegro form is invariably allegro in tempo and used exclusively in the first movement of the sonata cycle.

2. ....✔.... Sonata-allegro form is frequently used as the structural design for single-movement works.

3. .... All sonata-allegro movements are exactly alike in the disposition of the material.

4. ....✔.... The Theme and Variations and the Rondo frequently appear as independent compositions.

5. ....✔.... The Minuet has a middle section called the Trio.

6. ....✔.... Da Capo is the term used to designate the return to the beginning of a movement.

7. .... Nineteenth-century composers met the desire for a thematic connection between movements by the use of a cyclical structure.

NOTES

General Review III.   More Materials of Music

Match each item in Column II to its appropriate association in Column I

#	Column II	Column I		Options
1.	N Tonic	The tonal center of a key	A	Augmentation
2.	G Key	A group of related tones (no order implied) with a common center	B	Chromatic scale
3.	E Interval	The distance and relationship between any two tones	C	Diatonic
4.	I Octave	The distance from one tone to the next tone of the same name (above or below)	D	Diminution
5.	K Semitone ~~Tonic~~	The smallest intervallic unit in our musical system	E	Interval
6.	P Whole Tone	The interval encompassing two adjacent semitones	F	Inversion
7.	J Scale	A series of tones arranged in consecutive order (ascending or descending)	G	Key
8.	B Chromatic Scale	The twelve semitones of the octave arranged in consecutive order	H	Modulation
9.	O Transposition	The act of shifting all the tones of a composition a uniform distance to a higher or lower level of pitch	I	Octave
10.	H Modulation	The process of passing from one key to another	J	Scale
11.	C Diatonic	The general term that refers to major and minor scales and harmonies	K	Semitone
12.	M Theme	The basic idea in the construction of a musical work	L	Sequence
13.	L Sequence	The restatement of a musical idea at a higher or lower pitch level	M	Theme
14.	A Augmentation	The expansion of original note values into longer ones	N	Tonic
15.	D Diminution	The contraction of original note values into shorter ones	O	Transposition
16.	F Inversion	A musical idea turned upside down	P	Whole tone

(General Review III continued on page 58.)

17. Motive	The smallest fragment within a theme that forms a melodic-rhythmic unit	Coda
18. Sonata	A work consisting of a cycle of contrasting movements (involving sonata-allegro form) written for one or two instruments	Codetta
19. String Quartet a	A sonata for four string instruments	Concerto
20. Symphony b.	A sonata for orchestra	Cyclical Structure
21. Concerto c.	A sonata for solo instrument(s) and orchestra	Da Capo
22. Expo d	The first section of sonata-allegro form	Development
23. Dev e.	The second section of sonata-allegro form	Exposition
24. Rec f.	The third section of sonata-allegro form	Minuet
25. Codetta g	A small coda (the term usually applied to the closing section of the Exposition)	Motive
26. Coda	The final portion that completes a movement	Recapitulation
27. Sonata-Allegro h.	The representative form of the Classical period	Rondo
28. Theme & Var i.	A musical structure in which a theme is stated and then presented in a series of modifications	Rondo-Sonata
29. Minuet	A composition in triple meter, of dance origin, frequently serving as the third movement of the sonata cycle in the classical period	Scherzo
30. Scherzo j.	A composition that replaced the minuet as a movement of the nineteenth-century symphony	Sonata-allegro
31. Rondo k.	A form characterized by the recurrence of a principal theme group in alternation with contrasting sections	Sonata
32. Rondo-Sonata l.	A design that combines the spirit of the rondo with the structural characteristics of sonata-allegro form	String Quartet
33. Trio m.	The middle section of a Minuet or Scherzo	Symphony
34. Da Capo n.	The term used to designate the return to the beginning of a movement	Theme and Variations
35. Cyclical Structure o.	The recurrence of the same thematic material in various movements of a composition	Trio

Part Four

EIGHTEENTH-CENTURY CLASSICISM

Study Guide 16

CHAPTERS 14, 15, R50/S41, R51/S42

Although none of the characteristics below are exlusively related to any one period or style, each of them is prominently associated with either the classical or romantic period. Check the appropriate column indicating the <u>primary</u> association.

1. General characteristics:

	CHECK (✔)	
	CLASSICAL	**ROMANTIC**
a) Strangeness, wonder, ecstacy	....	....
b) The fanciful and the picturesque	....	....
c) Idealization of the cultures of ancient Greece and Rome	✓	....
d) Objectivity: self-detachment rather than egocentricity	✓	....
e) Intense subjectivity: art regarded primarily as a means of self-expression	....	....
f) Order, stability, control, moderation, discipline	✓	....
g) Aristocratic patronage of the arts	✓	....
h) Balanced proportions and finely wrought detail	✓	....
i) Idealization of the culture of the Middle Ages	....	....
j) Universality: international character of artistic expression	✓	....
k) Expressive content projected by means that tend toward extremes	....	....
l) Preoccupation with exotic atmosphere	....	....
m) Preoccupation with nationalism and local color	....	....
n) Balance between emotion and intellect	✓	....

2. Musical characteristics:

	CLASSICAL	ROMANTIC
a) The Church, the aristocratic salon and the opera house were the chief centers of public musical activity	✔	
b) Moderate-sized orchestra	✔	
c) Improved instruments; bigger orchestras; better players; expanded sonorities	✔	
d) The concert hall was the chief center of public musical activity	✔	
e) Moderate range of dynamics	✔	
f) Dynamics tend toward extremes in range		
g) Orchestration attains the status of a self-sufficient art		
h) Expansion of inherited instrumental forms (sonata cycle)	✔	
i) A tendency toward a union of the arts; a preoccupation with extramusical (programmatic) associations		
j) Transparency; delicate sonorities	✔	
k) The symphony and solo concerto become the most important types of absolute, orchestral music	✔	

CHAPTERS R50/S41, R51/S42

Check (✔) the correct completions:

1. The artist of the classical period addressed himself chiefly to

.... a working-class audience

....✔...... an aristocratic audience

2. Music created by eighteenth-century composers

.... was rarely performed in their lifetime

....✔...... was written for immediate performance

3. The patronage system

.... was without benefit to artists

....✔...... offered important advantages to those artists who successfully adjusted to it

4. The positive aspects of the patronage system are best exemplified in the career of

.... Dvořák   ....✔...... Haydn   .... Mozart   .... Schubert

5. The four masters of the classical Viennese school of composition were:

.... Verdi   .... Tchaikovsky   ....✔...... Schubert   ....✔...... Haydn

....✔...... Beethoven   .... Wagner   ....✔...... Mozart   .... Chopin

6. The full complement of the eighteenth-century orchestra numbered about

.... 15 players   ....✔...... 35 players   .... 75 players   .... 100 players

CHAPTER R51/S42

1. The classical period is identified with significant contributions to the art of music. Check (✔) those statements that describe these contributions:

a) .... Abolition of the major-minor system

b) ....✔........ Establishment of the sonata cycle as the most important type of absolute music

c) ....✔........ Development of opera buffa (comic opera)

d) ....✔........ Standardization of the sections of the orchestra in its modern arrangement of four basic choirs

e) .... Establishment of a scheme of dynamics that avoided crescendo and diminuendo

f) ....✔........ Devices of early operatic music: abrupt alterations of dynamics, sudden accents, tremolo, pizzicato, etc., added to the classical orchestral style

g) ....✔........ Establishment of the piano as the major keyboard instrument

h) .... Establishment of the harpsichord as the major keyboard instrument

i) ....✔........ The piano sonata becomes the most ambitious form of solo instrumental music

j) ....✔........ The creation of a universal style based on the Italian opera and Viennese symphony

2. Underline the correct word or phrase in parentheses that accurately completes each statement:

a) Composers of the Viennese classical school (were) (were not) flexible and experimental in their treatment of musical form.

b) In the music of the classical period, emotional expression (is) (is not) subordinated to "rules" of form.

c) The classical era in music (did) (did not) follow the classical era in literature and painting.   In time

d) Romantic qualities (are) (are not) present in music of the classical period.

3. In summary, "On the one hand classical art captured the exquisite refinement of a way of life that was drawing to a close. On the other it caught the intimations of a new way of life that was struggling to be born." This age encompassed a number of trends. The following list may serve to suggest some points of discussion:

1. Enlightened despotism

2. Doctrine of the divine right of kings

3. Twilight of the *ancien régime*

4. Industrial Revolution

5. The French *Encyclopédie*

6. Age of Reason

7. Augustan Age

8. *Sturm und Drang* — first outcroppings of romantic spirit

Complete the following statements:

1. The literature of the classical period abounds in a type of intimate ensemble music called ...Chamber... music.

2. Chamber music involves a performing group of from ...two... to ...8... players, with one player to each part.

3. The ensemble that held the central position in classical chamber music was the ...string... ...quartet...

4. The instruments comprising the string quartet are: ...1ˢᵗ violin..., ...2ⁿᵈ violins..., ...viola..., and ...cello...

5. The duo sonata was frequently scored for ...piano... and ...violin...

6. The instruments comprising the classical trio are: ...piano... ...violin... ...cello...

Notes

Study Guide 17

Miscellaneous Terms

CHAPTERS R52/S43, R53/S44

1. In opera and oratorio, a kind of musical declamation that follows the inflection of speech and is accompanied by the harpsichord is called .... (p. R262/S211)

2. The more melodious and expressive recitative accompanied by orchestra is called .... (p. R262/S211)

3. The Italian term that refers to the whole orchestra is .... (p. R264/S212)

4. A theme based on an upward-bounding arpeggio identified with the classical era is called a .... (p. R269/S217)

Notes

AURAL ANALYSIS
A Comparison of Styles: Classic vs. Romantic

<table>
<tr><td align="center">I.</td><td align="center">II.</td></tr>
<tr><td>Mozart: SYMPHONY NO. 40 in G MINOR, K. 550
— Fourth Movement</td><td>Wagner: THE FLYING DUTCHMAN
— OVERTURE</td></tr>
</table>

Or others of your choice:

Composition	Composition ....
Composer	Composer ....

1. Check (✔) the attributes that are prominently displayed in each composition.

		I.	II.
Melody:	....	Extended line(s) of a marked lyrical nature	.... Extended line(s) of a marked lyrical nature
	✔	Moderately lyrical	.... Moderately lyrical
Dynamics:	....	Wide range; exploitation of extremes	.... Wide range; exploitation of extremes
	✔	Moderate range predominates	.... Moderate range predominates
Pitch:	....	Wide range; exploitation of extremes	.... Wide range; exploitation of extremes
	✔	Moderate range predominates	.... Moderate range predominates
Timbre:	....	Wide variety	.... Wide variety
	✔	Moderate variety	.... Moderate variety
Orchestra:	....	Large size	.... Large size
	✔	Moderate size	.... Moderate size
Sonority:	....	Tends toward a rich, colorful sound	.... Tends toward a rich, colorful sound
	✔	Tends toward a light, sparse sound	.... Tends toward a light, sparse sound
Tempo:	....	Fluctuates conspicuously within a movement	.... Fluctuates conspicuously within a movement
	✔	Fairly constant within a movement	.... Fairly constant within a movement
Expressive content:	✔	Projected by the materials of music within a relatively moderate range	.... Projected by the materials of music within a relatively moderate range
	....	Projected by the materials of music within a relatively expanded range	.... Projected by the materials of music within a relatively expanded range

2. Composition I is representative of the ....*Class*............................ period.

3. Composition II is representative of the .... period.

4. With respect to each period, list other stylistic attributes that may be present in each composition:

.........*lyrical melodies*....................	....
.........*sonata-alleg. form*..............	....
.........*diatonic harmonies*............	....

AURAL ANALYSIS
A Comparison of Styles: Classic vs. Romantic

I.   II.

Composition ....   Composition ....

Composer ....   Composer ....

1. Check (✔) the attributes that are prominently displayed in each composition.

		I.	II.
Melody:	....	Extended line(s) of a marked lyrical nature	.... Extended line(s) of a marked lyrical nature
	....	Moderately lyrical	.... Moderately lyrical
Dynamics:	....	Wide range; exploitation of extremes	.... Wide range; exploitation of extremes
	....	Moderate range predominates	.... Moderate range predominates
Pitch:	....	Wide range; exploitation of extremes	.... Wide range; exploitation of extremes
	....	Moderate range predominates	.... Moderate range predominates
Timbre:	....	Wide variety	.... Wide variety
	....	Moderate variety	.... Moderate variety
Orchestra:	....	Large size	.... Large size
	....	Moderate size	.... Moderate size
Sonority:	....	Tends toward a rich, colorful sound	.... Tends toward a rich, colorful sound
	....	Tends toward a light, sparse sound	.... Tends toward a light, sparse sound
Tempo:	....	Fluctuates conspicuously within a movement	.... Fluctuates conspicuously within a movement
	....	Fairly constant within a movement	.... Fairly constant within a movement
Expressive content:	....	Projected by the materials of music within a relatively moderate range	.... Projected by the materials of music within a relatively moderate range
	....	Projected by the materials of music within a relatively expanded range	.... Projected by the materials of music within a relatively expanded range

2. Composition I is representative of the .... period.

3. Composition II is representative of the .... period.

4. With respect to each period, list other stylistic attributes that may be present in each composition:

....

....

....

THE SONATA CYCLE
Guided Listening — Aural Analysis

In listening to music, the esthetic experience is enhanced by an awareness of the musical form. The following listening aids are designed to offer assistance in grasping the structural elements of four forms often found in the classical sonata cycle:

1. Sonata-allegro
2. Theme and Variations
3. Minuet and Trio
4. Rondo

Each form will be dealt with in two ways:

1. A *Listening Guide* is designed to lead the student through a movement by pointing out and describing significant musical events as they occur.

2. An *Aural Analysis* outline calls upon the student to make determinations with respect to musical events as they occur.

The accumulated experience will serve to strengthen perceptive listening and understanding of musical form.

In the *Aural Analysis* outlines, statements indicated by ⟶ are guideposts, intended to assist the student in following the course of music. Bar references to the score are supplied in the Appendix.

N.B. For instructions on the use of Listening Guides and Aural Analysis outlines, refer to page iv.

LISTENING GUIDE

Mozart: SYMPHONY NO. 41, IN C MAJOR, K. 551, ("Jupiter")

Movement:	First
Key:	C major
Tempo:	Allegro vivace
Meter:	Quadruple ($\frac{4}{4}$)
Instrumentation:	1 Flute, 2 Oboes, 2 Bassoons, 2 Horns, 2 Trumpets, 2 Timpani, Violins, Violas, Cellos, Double Basses.

EXPOSITION

First Theme Group
(Home Key: C major)

1. Stately; tutti (*f*) vs. strings (*p*).

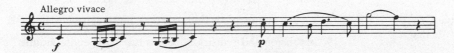

2. Expansion: tutti (*f*). First Theme Group ends with a FERMATA (HOLD: ⌢).

3. Theme restated (strings) with a countermelody (woodwinds).

4. Transition: tutti (*f*); chordal cadence. Moment of SILENCE.

Second Theme Group
(Contrasting Key: G major)

5. Lyrical; strings (*p*). Ends staccato, high register. SILENCE.

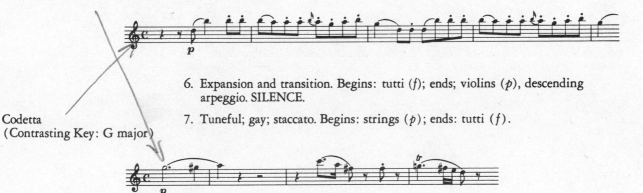

6. Expansion and transition. Begins: tutti (*f*); ends; violins (*p*), descending arpeggio. SILENCE.

7. Tuneful; gay; staccato. Begins: strings (*p*); ends: tutti (*f*).

Codetta
(Contrasting Key: G major)

(The Exposition may be repeated.)

DEVELOPMENT
(Free Modulation)

8. Four-note *modulation*; woodwinds (*p*).

9. Codetta theme explored; frequent shifts of tonal areas.

10. Sequential imitation: high vs. low registers; activity; tension.

11. First Theme Group presented (*p*).

12. Fragments of First Theme explored (*f*).

13. Transition: staccato (*p*); woodwinds featured.

RECAPITULATION

(Exposition substantially restated.)

First Theme Group
(Home Key: C major)

14. Stately; tutti (*f*) vs. strings (*p*).

15. Expansion: tutti (*f*). First theme group ends with a FERMATA.

16. Theme with countermelody restated in minor key.

17. Transition: tutti (*f*); chordal cadence. SILENCE.

Second Theme Group
(Home Key: C major)

18. Lyrical; strings (*p*). Ends staccato, high register. SILENCE.

19. Expansion and transition. Begins tutti (*f*); ends: violins (*p*), descending arpeggio. SILENCE.

Coda
(Home Key: C major)

20. Tuneful; gay; staccato. Begins: strings (*p*); ends: tutti (*f*).

AURAL ANALYSIS
Sonata-Allegro

Mozart: SYMPHONY NO. 40, IN G MINOR, K. 550

Movement: (First)
Key: G minor
Tempo: Molto allegro
Meter: Duple (¢)
Instrumentation: 1 Flute, 2 Oboes, 2 Clarinets, 2 Bassoons, 2 Horns, Violins, Violas, Cellos, Double Basses.

EXPOSITION

First Theme Group
(Home Key: G minor)

Check (✔)

1. Begins: ......✓...... strings, *p*; long melodic line

.... woodwinds, *f*; chords, staccato

2. First Theme restated and expanded: .....✗..... Yes .... No

→ 3. Cadence, *f*. SILENCE.

Second Theme Group
(Contrasting key: B-flat major)

4. ......✓...... Section marked by lyricism; dialogue; *p*: strings-woodwinds

.... Section marked by turbulence; tutti, *f*.

→ 5. Section ends with descending scale, staccato

Codetta
(Contrasting key: B-flat major)

6. .... Based on new material

.....✗...... Based on First Theme (opening three-note motive)

→ 7. Cadence, *f*. Active violin figure vs. chords

(The Exposition may be repeated.)

DEVELOPMENT

8. This section includes:

	YES	NO
a) Reference to First Theme	✗	
b) Reference to Second Theme		✗
c) Shifts in tonal areas (**Modulation**)	✗	
d) Sequential passages	✓	
e) Contrasting registers and timbres	✓	

→ 9. Final measures: flute, clarinets — descending sequence; bassoons — pedal point

RECAPITULATION

First Theme Group
(Home Key: G minor)

10. Begins: .... Woodwinds, *f*

.......✗... Strings, *p*

11. Expansion and transition — developmental character:

.....✗..... Yes .... No

→ 12. Cadence, *f*. SILENCE

Second Theme Group (Home Key: G minor)	13. .....X..... Section marked by lyricism; dialogue, *p*: strings-woodwinds
	.... Section marked by turbulence; tutti, *f*
→	14. Section ends with descending scale passage, staccato
Coda (Home Key: G minor)	15. Dominated by First Theme three-note motive:
	.....X..... Yes .... No

LISTENING GUIDE
Theme and Variations

Schubert: PIANO QUINTET IN A MAJOR, OPUS 114 ("Trout")

Movement:	Fourth
Key:	D major
Tempo:	Andantino
Meter:	Duple ($\frac{2}{4}$)
Instrumentation:	Violin, Viola, Cello, Double Bass, Piano.

Theme
Binary Form:
a − a − b

1. Strings only (*pp*).

Variation I   2. Theme presented by piano in octaves; accompaniment in the strings.

Variation II   3. Theme presented by viola with piano response; florid counterfigure in violin.

Variation III   4. Theme presented by cello and bass; florid counterfigure in piano.

Variation IV   5. Key change: D minor. Theme subjected to harmonic, rhythmic, and dynamic modifications.

Variation V   6. Key change: B-flat major. Modification of theme presented by cello; occasional commentary by piano and violin.

Variation VI   7. Key change: D major. Variation characterized by dispersal among various instruments of melody and original piano accompaniment.

AURAL ANALYSIS
Theme and Variations

Before proceeding with this aural analysis, listen to the entire theme so as to become acquainted with it.

Haydn: SYMPHONY NO. 94 IN G MAJOR, (*Surprise*)

Movement:	Second
Key:	C major
Tempo:	Andante
Meter:	Duple ($\frac{2}{4}$)
Instrumentation:	2 Flutes, 2 Oboes, 2 Bassoons, 2 Horns, 2 Trumpets, 2 Timpani, Violins, Violas, Cellos, Double Basses.

Check (✔)

Theme
Binary Form:
  A   B
a – a b – b

1. Mode: ....✔ Major   .... Minor

2. Dynamics predominantly: .... Forte   ✔ Piano

3. Articulation predominantly: ....✔ Staccato   .... Legato

4. Timbre: ....✔ Strings predominate   .... Brass predominates

Variation I

5. ....X.... Major mode   .... Minor mode

6. ....X.... Addition of countermelody   .... Theme in shorter note values

Variation II

7. .... Major mode   ....X.... Minor mode

8. New rhythmic and melodic treatment of *B*: .... Yes   ....X.... No

➡ 9. Short bridge — violins — leads to:

Variation III

10. ....X.... Major mode   .... Minor mode

11. ....✔.... Theme in shorter note values (sense of quicker movement)

    .... Theme in longer note values (sense of slower movement)

12. Theme with countermelody: ....X.... Yes   .... No

Variation IV

13. Theme in brass and woodwinds: ......X...... Yes   .... No

14. Syncopated chords in strings: ......X...... Yes   .... No

15. Rhythmic and melodic modification of theme: ......X...... Yes   .... No

16. ......X...... Major mode   .... Minor mode

➡ 17. Short extension (tutti) ends with fermata

Coda

18. ......X..... Theme recalled, *p*, mixed timbres; new harmonic coloration

    .... New material, *f*, strings only

LISTENING GUIDE
Minuet

Mozart: SYMPHONY No. 35 IN D MAJOR, K. 385 ("Haffner")

Movement:	Third
Key:	D major
Tempo:	Menuetto
Meter:	Triple ($\frac{3}{4}$)
Instrumentation:	2 Oboes, 2 Bassoons, 2 Horns, 2 Trumpets, 2 Timpani, Violins, Violas, Cellos, Double Basses.

Minuet   1. *a*   Tutti, *f*, arpeggios and chords vs. strings, *p*, syncopated figure.
(A)

      2. *a*   Repeated.

      3. *b*   Tutti, *f*, wide upward leaps in melody vs. strings, *p*, descending line.

      4. *a*   Restated.

      5. $\left.\begin{matrix} b \\ a \end{matrix}\right\}$ Repeated.

Trio   6. *c*   Melody in thirds dominated by woodwinds and violins.
(B)

      7. *c*   Repeated.

      8. *d*   Graceful melody in strings; pedal point in woodwinds and horns.

      9. *c*   Restated.

     10. $\left.\begin{matrix} d \\ c \end{matrix}\right\}$ Repeated.

Minuet   11. Da capo (from the beginning: *a-b-a* without repeats).
(A)

AURAL ANALYSIS
Minuet

30 pts.

p 471

Mozart: *Eine kleine Nachtmusik*, K. 525

Movement:	Third
Key:	G major
Tempo:	Allegretto
Meter:	Triple ($\frac{3}{4}$)
Instrumentation:	Violins, Violas, Cellos, Double Basses

Check (✔)

Minuet
(A)

1. *a* begins: .....X..... *f*, non-legato, processional

.... *p*, legato, flowing

2. *a* repeated: ....X..... Yes .... No

3. *b* begins: .... *f*, staccato. No reference to *a*

.....X..... *p*, legato. Ends with reference to *a*

4. *b* repeated: .....X..... Yes .... No

Trio
(B)

5. *c* ....X..... *p*, Violins I — solo character

.... *f*, Cellos play melodic line

6. *c* repeated: ....X..... Yes .... No

7. *d* .....X..... *f*, scalewise

.... *p*, solid chords

8. *c* restated: .....X..... Yes .... No

9. *d*⎫
   c⎭ repeated: ....X..... Yes .... No

Minuet
(A)

10. Da capo (from the beginning: *a-b-a* without repeats): .....X..... Yes .... No

73

LISTENING GUIDE
Rondo

Beethoven: PIANO SONATA IN C MINOR, Opus 13 ("Pathétique")

Movement:	Third (Finale)
Key:	C minor
Tempo:	Allegro
Meter:	Duple (¢)

Rondo Theme   1. Begins: *p* — light, sprightly melody in treble; arpeggiated accompaniment in bass.

(A)   Ends: chords, *f*. SILENCE.

         2. Short bridge: chords, arpeggios, sequence.

Episode   3. *Dolce* — syncopations, scale passages, running triplet figure. Cadence.
(B)

Codetta   4. Begins: *p* — repeated chords, staccato.
            Ends: *ff* — descending scale-sweep to a sustained chord.

Rondo Theme   5. Exact restatement.
(A)

Episode   6. New theme: Larger note values (*p*, legato)
(C)   Syncopations
                           Theme counterposed to running scales
                           (*p* ⟍ *f*, staccato).
                           Dominant pedal point vs. arpeggios.
                           ff — descending scale-sweep to a sustained chord.

Rondo Theme   7. Modified restatement (abbreviated).
(A)

Episode   8. Modified restatement.
(B)

Codetta   9. Modified restatement leads to

Rondo Theme   10. Modified restatement.
(A)

Coda   11. Triplet figures
                      Syncopated chords
                      Descending scale-sweep
                      Rondo theme recalled
                      Close, *ff*.

AURAL ANALYSIS
Rondo

Mozart: HORN CONCERTO IN E-FLAT MAJOR, K. 447

Movement:	Third (Finale)
Key:	E-flat major
Tempo:	Allegro
Meter:	Sextuple ($\frac{6}{8}$)
Instrumentation:	2 Clarinets, 2 Bassoons, Solo horn, Violins, Violas, Cellos, Double Basses.

Check (✔)

Rondo Theme Group (A)

1. .... Solo horn; lively

.... Solo clarinet; tranquil

2. Theme restated and expanded: .... Yes .... No

→ 3. Cadence: chords, *f*. SILENCE.

First Episode (B)

4. Characterized by:

.... Melody of lyrical nature

.... Interplay — solo horn and orchestra

.... Absence of solo instrument

.... Hunting call figure present

→ 5. Short bridge leads to:

6. .... Rondo theme group (A)

.... Restatement of first episode (B)

.... New episode (C)

→ 7. Short bridge leads to:

8. .... Rondo theme group (A)

.... Restatement of first episode (B)

.... New episode (C)

→ 9. Short bridge leads to:

10. .... Rondo theme group (A)

.... Restatement of first episode (B)

.... New episode (C)

Outline the form of this rondo with appropriate letters taken from the analysis:

....

General Review IV.   Eighteenth-Century Classicism

With respect to music of the classical period, match each item in the following list to its appropriate association:

Aristocratic patronage   Opera buffa   Sonata cycle

Chamber music   Orchestra   Universality

Church, aristocratic   Order, stability,
salon, opera house   discipline

Crescendo-diminuendo   Piano

1. ....
   .... } General qualities that pervade the art of this period
   ....

2. .... The main source of economic support for the musician

3. .... A designation pertaining to a high degree of homogeneity of style and the international character of art

4. .... The outstanding type of comic opera

5. ....
   .... } The chief centers of public musical activity
   ....

6. .... The multi-movement genre that was pre-eminent

7. .... The instrumental ensemble that acquired a standardized arrangement in four basic choirs

8. .... Gradations in dynamics that became prominent

9. .... The major keyboard instrument

10. .... A popular type of intimate ensemble music, with one player to each part

Part Five

MEDIEVAL, RENAISSANCE, AND BAROQUE MUSIC

Study Guide 18

CHAPTER R57/S48

I. Complete the following:

1. The general term pertaining to a musical fabric is ....

2. An individual musical line (vocal or instrumental) is called a ....

3. Single-voiced texture is ....

4. Many-voiced texture is ....

5. The art of combining two or more musical lines, each with a rhythmic life of its own, is called

   ....

6. A non-contrapuntal texture in which a single melodic line is conceived in relation to a harmonic background

   is ....

II. Check (✔) the true statements:

1. .... Melody constitutes the horizontal aspect of music.

2. .... Harmony constitutes the vertical aspect of music.

3. .... A composition must be exclusively of one texture.

4. .... From 1000 to 1600, music was predominantly polyphonic.

5. .... Since 1600, polyphony and homophony have existed concurrently.

6. .... Throughout the classical and romantic periods, composers emphasized the contrapuntal aspect of music.

7. .... During the twentieth century, composers have re-explored and utilized the contrapuntal process (independent part writing).

III. The following compositional techniques occur frequently in contrapuntal writing.

Match each of the following to its appropriate association:

Augmentation   Diminution   Inversion   Round

Canon   Imitation   Retrograde

1. .... A subject or motive presented in one voice and then restated in another
2. .... The strictest type of imitation in which the whole length of a musical line is restated in another voice
3. .... A vocal canon at the unison or octave
4. .... The original melody turned upside down
5. .... The notes of the original theme in longer time values
6. .... The notes of the original theme in shorter time values
7. .... The notes of the original theme in reverse order

IV. The following is the beginning of the familiar round *Frère Jacques*:

In each example below, the original is subjected to a different compositional process. Identify:

Augmentation — Diminution — Imitation — Inversion — Retrograde

1. ....

2. ....

3. ....

4. ....

5. ....

CHAPTER R58/S49

V. Check (✔) the block in which every reference is correctly related to Gregorian chant.

1. ....

Identified with the Christian Church
Pope Gregory the Great
Plainsong
Monophonic
Latin texts
Well-known composers
Subjected to changes
Wide melodic leaps
Extreme dynamic contrasts
Handed down orally
Modal melodies

2. ....

Identified with the Christian Church
Greek, Hebrew and Syrian influences
Pope Gregory the Great
Plainsong
Monophonic
Latin texts
Free-verse rhythm
Anonymous melodies
Handed down orally
Utilized neumes
Modal melodies

3. ....

Greek, Hebrew and Syrian influences
Pope Gregory the Great
Homophonic
Text in the vernacular
Free-verse rhythm
Subjected to changes
Regular phrase structure
Handed down orally
Utilized neumes
Secular texts
Tonal melodies

4. ....

Greek, Hebrew and Syrian influences
Identified with the Christian Church
Pope Gregory the Great
Plainsong
Polyphonic
Latin texts
Regular accents
Free-verse rhythm
Handed down orally
Utilized neumes
Sacred texts

TEXTURE — ANALYSIS

The following compositions are recorded in *Masterpieces of Music before 1750* (Haydn Society). Identify the texture that predominates in each composition. Where more than one texture is evident, indicate accordingly.

	CHECK (✔)		
	MONOPHONIC	**CONTRAPUNTAL**	**HOMOPHONIC**
1. Sequence, *Victimae Paschali* (Gregorian)	....	....	....
2. *Christ lag in Todesbanden*, Chorale (Bach)	....	....	....
3. Sanctus from the *Missa prolationum* (Ockeghem)	....	....	....
4. Sonata in C minor (D. Scarlatti)	....	....	....
5. *Ricercar dopo il Credo* (Frescobaldi)	....	....	....
6. Alleluia, *Vidimus stellam* (Gregorian)	....	....	....
Others of your choice:			
7.	....	....	....
8.	....	....	....
9.	....	....	....
10.	....	....	....

Notes

Study Guide 19

CHAPTER R59/S49

Complete the following:

1. The most important development in the history of Western music took place in the Romanesque period (c. 850-1150): the emergence of .... texture as a stylistic factor.

2. With the advent of polyphony, several momentous developments took place in music:

   a) The emergence of regular ...., which enabled the different voices to keep together;

   b) The development of the modern ...., whose lines and spaces (in conjunction with a clef) made possible the indication of exact ....;

   c) The invention of a system of note symbols that indicated the .... of each sound.

3. The Gothic era (c. 1150-1450) saw a flourishing of secular music in the art of the .... and ....

4. Composers of the Gothic era constructed extended musical works through the various devices of ....

5. The earliest kind of polyphonic music is called ....

6. Two outstanding composers of the Notre Dame school (late twelfth and early thirteenth centuries) were .... and ....

7. The five sections of the Mass that are most commonly set to music are the ...., ..., ..., ..., ...

8. The Latin term referring to the *fixed melody* upon which composers generally based their polyphonic settings of the Mass is ....

9. The Mass for the Dead is called ....

10. At the beginning of the fourteenth century a new musical style emerged known as the ....

11. The outstanding composer of the *ars nova* was ....

12. Fifteenth-century composers of the Burgundian school:

 a) frequently based all movements of their Mass compositions on the same ....;

 b) used voices in .... register;

 c) used a mixture of contrasting instruments such as ....

 ....;

 d) supplemented the intervals of the fourth and fifth with the intervals of the ....

 and ....;

 e) fashioned .... melodies and .... rhythms;

 f) foreshadowed a harmonic language based on ...., ...

 ...., and a sense of ....

13. The most renowned composer of the Burgundian school was ...., one of the first to use secular melodies in his religious works.

Notes

Study Guide 20

Items preceded by an asterisk (*) are for use with the Regular Version only.

CHAPTER R60/S50, R61

I. Complete the following:

1. The .... period (c. 1450-1600) marks the passing of European society from

   an exclusively religious to a more .... orientation.

2. The Renaissance found its inspiration in the cultures of ancient .... and

   ....

3. The country in which the Renaissance originated was ....

II. Check (✔) those references that relate to the esthetic ideals manifested in Renaissance art:

1. .... Unquestioning faith and mysticism

2. .... Belief in reason and scientific inquiry

3. .... Reliance on evidence of the senses

4. .... Reliance on tradition and authority

5. .... Concern for harmonious proportions

6. .... Interest in the human form

7. .... Love of nature

8. .... Preoccupation with laws of perspective and composition

9. .... Portrayal of life as an allegory

10. .... Inclination toward realism

11. .... A heightened awareness of the human personality

III. Check (✔) the references that are correct with respect to characteristics of sixteenth-century music:

1. .... Clarity, simplicity, and sensuous appeal

2. .... Accompanied choral music predominates

3. .... The golden age of a cappella style

4. .... Homophonic texture emphasized

5. .... Principle of continuous imitation prevails

6. .... Contrapuntal texture

IV. Match each of the following items to its appropriate association:

A cappella   Ayre   Antiphonal   Ballett
Continuous Imitation Madrigal   Motet   Ritornello

1. .... A term that denotes a vocal work without instrumental accompaniment

2. .... Reiterated statements of motives or themes in various vocal lines (a principle that governed Renaissance polyphony)

3. .... A choral work, with or without accompaniment, of either sacred or secular character, intended to be performed at religious or festive occasions

4. .... A style, originating in Venice, characterized by groups of singers and players performing in alternation (p. R337/S264)

*5. .... A musical refrain that returns throughout a work (p. R338)

6. .... One of the chief forms of Renaissance secular vocal music, whose text dealt with such diverse topics as love, satire, and political themes (pp. R340/S261-262)

7. .... The old English name for a song or aria (p. R345/S265)

8. .... A type of English madrigal, strophic in structure, with the character of a dance-song (p. R346/S265)

V. Match each of the composers listed to his appropriate association:

Byrd   Gabrieli, G.   Lassus   Morley
Dowland   Gesualdo   Marenzio   Palestrina
Gabrieli, A.   Josquin des Prez

1. ....
   .... Two pre-eminent composers of the Flemish school (pp. R330, 331/ S258, 264)

2. .... Italian composer (of the Roman school) who met the need for a reformed church music in the sixteenth century (p. R334/S260)

3. ....
   .... The two outstanding composers of the Venetian school (p. R338/ S264)

4. .... Regarded as the greatest master of the Italian madrigal (p. R340/S262)

5. .... An Italian madrigalist noted for his innovations in chromatic harmony (p. R341/S264)

6. ....
   .... Three outstanding English composers of the Elizabethan period (pp. R343, 344, 345/S264, 265)
   ....

NAME .... CLASS .... DATE ....

Study Guide 21

Items preceded by an asterisk (*) are for use with the Regular Version only.

CHAPTER R62/S51

Check (✔) those qualities that are prominently represented in baroque art (c. 1600-1750):

1. .... Boldness of gesture

2. .... Vigor, turbulence

3. .... Avoidance of the dramatic

4. .... Color and movement

5. .... Tension of opposing masses

6. .... Pathos

7. .... Splendor, opulence, sensuous beauty

8. .... Lack of concern with religious themes

9. .... Mysticism

10. .... Theatricality

11. .... Grandiosity, monumentality

CHAPTERS R63/S52, R65/S53

Complete the following statements:

*1. The early baroque solo song with instrumental accompaniment is called ....

*2. Monody has a .... texture.

*3. The monodic style emerged about .... A.D.

4. The attempts of the Florentine Camerata to resurrect the musical-dramatic art of ancient ....
   led to the invention of ....

5. The new representational style (*stile rappresentativo*) consisted of a .... that
   moved freely over a foundation of simple ....

6. The first complete opera, ..., with a libretto by ....
   and music by ...., was first presented in Florence, Italy, in the year ....

7. The composer of *Orfeo* (1607), who developed and enriched the innovations of the Camerata, was ....
   .... (pp. R361, 363/S277)

Match each of the following items to its appropriate association with respect to baroque music:

Basso continuo	Figured bass	Minor
Basso ostinato	Ground bass	Rhythm
Binary form	Improvisation	Terraced dynamics
Continuous melody	Instrumental music	Thorough-bass
Doctrine of the affections	Major	Virtuosity
Equal temperament	Melismatic	Well-Tempered Clavier

1. ....
....
....
} Three designations for the practice that involves the "realization" of a bass line

2. ....
....
} The modes that replaced the church modes as the basis for melodic and harmonic structure in Western music

3. .... An adjustment in tuning that divides the octave into twelve equal intervals

4. .... The title of Bach's keyboard work in two volumes, each of which contains a prelude and fugue in every one of the twelve major and twelve minor keys

5. .... A common practice that involved word-tone painting in vocal music and the prevalence of a single mood within each movement of an instrumental piece

6. .... A manner of word setting in which a single syllable is set to an extended melodic line

7. .... The element of music that in many works manifests a steady, unflagging drive

8. .... The principle of continuous expansion, by which a melodic line unfolds through a process of ceaseless spinning out

9. .... A characteristic feature resulting from two alternating levels of tonal volume

10. .... A structural design that played an important role in music of this period

11. ....
....
} Two designations for a short musical phrase persistently repeated in the bass while the upper parts pursue varying courses (p. S279)

12. .... A branch of the art that gained in importance comparable to that of vocal music

13. .... A term referring to prodigious technical mastery in instrumental and vocal performance

14. .... The practice of spontaneous extemporization in performance

CHAPTERS R63, 64/S52

I. Check (✔) the true statements:

1. .... The earliest Florentine composers of opera brought music and poetry into a close relationship. [Their aim was to heighten the emotional power of the text.]

2. .... The new operatic form, freed of the complexities of counterpoint, relied on a homophonic texture.

3. .... Dissonant harmonies are found only in music of the nineteenth century.

4. .... In order to accommodate necessary musical expansion, baroque composers of vocal music engaged in the practice of repeating lines, phrases and individual words of the text.

5. .... Dance rhythms were native to the spirit and practice of baroque music.

6. .... Sweeping crescendos and diminuendos were characteristic of the Baroque.

7. .... Baroque improvisation was an art practiced by both vocalists and instrumentalists.

II. Complete the following with respect to the Baroque:

1. The instrument that supplanted the viol was the ....

2. Two popular brass instruments were the .... and ....

3. Three popular woodwind instruments were the ...., ..., and ....

4. The three important keyboard instruments were the ...., ..., and ....

5. The word used in Germany as the general term for a keyboard instrument is ....

Notes

Study Guide 22

CHAPTER 66 (Regular Version only)

Complete the following:

1. The formal or serious opera of the Baroque was called ....

2. The artificial male soprano and alto singers of early eighteenth-century opera were known as ....

3. The development of music in all its branches (vocal and instrumental) was nourished by baroque ....

4. Four vocal components developed in baroque opera are:

   ...., ..., ..., ...

5. The da capo aria was influential in establishing .... form as a basic formula of musical structure.

6. In the Baroque, the center for new trends and experiments in music was the ....

7. Two pre-eminent middle baroque composers were .... (1632-87), active in France; and .... (1659-95), in England.

8. Lully is particularly associated with the development of the .... overture.

CHAPTER 67 (Regular Version only)

Complete the following:

1. Out of a fusion of sixteenth-century vocal polyphony and baroque opera came two important forms:

   .... and ....

2. The first oratorios were sacred music dramas and were produced as ....

3. Baroque oratorio is a large-scale musical work for ...., ..., and ...., based as a rule on a ....

4. Although similar to opera, oratorios are presented without ...., ..., or ....

5. Four operatic vocal components found in the oratorio and cantata are:

   ...., ..., ..., ...

CHAPTER R68/S54

I. Check (✔) the true statements:

1. The sonata da camera:

    a) is basically .... a suite of stylized dances

    .... a suite in which each piece has the same tempo and mood

    b) was intended for performance .... in the church

    .... in secular surroundings

2. The sonata da chiesa:

    a) was intended for performance .... in the church

    .... in secular surroundings

    b) is .... more contrapuntal in texture than the sonata da camera

    .... less contrapuntal in texture than the sonata da camera

3. The trio sonata (da camera; da chiesa):

    a) .... was composed for two violins and continuo

    b) .... is performed by three instrumentalists

    c) .... is performed by four instrumentalists

II. Complete the following:

1. A type of composition that features a small group of instruments opposed to a larger group is called

   ....

2. The style based on the principle of the opposition of two dissimilar masses of sound is known as

   .... style.

3. In the concerto grosso, the small group is called the ....; the large group is

   called the .... or ....

4. The opposing forces in the concerto grosso create alternating levels of sound volume, known as

   ....

5. In the concerto grosso, the keyboard instrument that furnishes harmonic support for both groups is the

   ....

6. Two early Italian masters of the concertante style were .... (1653-1713) and

   .... (1678-1741).

CHAPTER R68/S55

III. Underline the correct word that appropriately completes each statement with respect to the baroque suite:

1. Its overall structure is	single-movement	multi-movement
2. Rhythms are derived chiefly from	song	dance
3. The key of each movement is	identical	different
4. The national origins of the type of dances are	homogeneous	heterogeneous
5. The predominant structural design of the individual movements is	binary	ternary

NAME .... CLASS .... DATE ....

Study Guide 23

Items preceded by an asterisk (*) are for use with the Regular Version only.

CHAPTER R69/S55

Complete the following:

1. The texture of the fugue is ....

2. The fugue is based on the principle of ....

3. The several musical lines of a fugue are called ....

4. In the opening section of a fugue:

   a) the theme, when first stated (in the tonic), is called the ....

   b) the theme, in its second entrance (dominant), is called the ....

   c) the theme, if introduced a third time (tonic), is called the ....

   d) the theme, if introduced a fourth time (dominant), is called the ....

   e) the counterpoint attending the *answer* is called the ....

5. The first section of a fugue, which consists of the initial presentation of the theme in each of the voices, is called the ....

6. The interludes that alternate with the sections emphasizing the subject are called ....

7. The fugue embodies the principle of the opposition between .... and .... keys.

8. The device of introducing the theme in one voice before its statement has been completed in another is called ....

9. A sustained tone (usually in the bass) held against harmonic changes in the other parts is called a ....

10. The only section of the fugue that follows a set order is the ....

11. A quasi-fugal passage in a nonfugal piece is known as ....

*12. A baroque form (derived from an old Spanish dance) that utilized the principle of the ground bass is the ....

*13. The passacaglia is a theme with variations. The theme is introduced in the .... voice, and remains there during most of the variations. (The variations are usually presented in the upper voices.)

*14. The theme of the passacaglia is usually .... or .... bars long and in .... meter.

*15. A baroque type related to the passacaglia is the ....

*16. In the passacaglia, the variations are based on a melody; in the chaconne, the variations are based on a succession of .... repeated throughout the composition.

93

CHAPTER R70/S55

Complete the following:

1. The da capo aria is structured according to the principle of .... form.

2. The baroque aria is frequently conceived as a duet between the .... and a ....

....

3. In baroque vocal music, the secco recitative is usually accompanied by the .... or

....; the accompagnato, is supported by the ....

4. A hymn tune associated with German Protestantism is known as a ....

5. The innovator who introduced congregational participation in religious services through the use of the chorale was

.... (1485-1546).

6. Four sources from which the Lutheran chorales were adapted are:

....

....

7. The chorale, with the melody in the soprano voice, strenthened the trend toward .... texture.

8. The musical setting of that portion of the Gospels which deals with the suffering and death of Christ is called

.... (p. R387/S289)

Notes

Study Guide 24

CHAPTER R72/S57

I. Check (✔) the correct completions:

1. The baroque prelude:

.... is based on the continuous expansion of a single melodic or rhythmic figure.

.... is based on the development of contrasting ideas.

2. The toccata:

a) is a composition for .... orchestra

.... a keyboard instrument

b) has a form that is .... free (rhapsodic)

.... prescribed

c) is predicated on .... virtuoso performance

.... the figured bass

3. The fantasia:

a) relies on .... a prescribed structure

.... the spirit of improvisation

b) involves .... changes of mood

.... a single affection

c) usually contains .... no embellishments

.... ample ornamentation

4. The chorale prelude and chorale variations were extensions and elaborations of

.... original melodies

.... traditional hymn tunes

5. The French overture:

a) is patterned on the sequence of .... slow-fast-slow

.... fast-slow-fast

b) contains .... a fast fugal section

.... no fugal section

6. The Italian overture:

a) is patterned on the sequence of .... slow-fast-slow

.... fast-slow-fast

b) contains .... a fugal section

.... no fugal section

7. The invention:

    a) is usually a   .... short piece

                                  .... piece of extended length

    b) is a piece for   .... a keyboard instrument

                                  .... solo instrument and orchestra

    c) is predominantly   .... homophonic

                                  .... contrapuntal

II. Identify the period most closely associated with each of the following stylistic tendencies:

	CHECK (✔)	
	CLASSICAL	BAROQUE
1. A widespread interest in religious music	....	....
2. Equal importance to instrumental and vocal music	....	....
3. Instrumental music assumes the dominant role	....	....
4. Predominant interest in homophonic texture	....	....
5. The individual movement usually based on one theme and mood	....	....
6. The individual movement usually based on contrasting themes and moods	....	....
7. A single, persistent figure tends to dominate the rhythm of a movement	....	....
8. A movement usually contains a variety of rhythmic patterns	....	....
9. A preference for mixed timbres and continual changes of tone color	....	....
10. Single instrumental colors chosen to stand out against an orchestral or vocal tonal mass	....	....
11. Improvisation — an essential element of performance	....	....
12. Improvisation — limited to the cadenza in the concerto	....	....
13. Performer's realization of the figured bass	....	....
14. All parts fully written out by the composer	....	....
15. Instrumentation and dynamics specified in the score	....	....
16. Choice of instruments and dynamics often left to the discretion of the performer	....	....
17. The format of the orchestra stabilized in four sections	....	....
18. The harpsichord — a basic member of the orchestra	....	....
19. The function of the harpsichord in the orchestra taken over by other instruments	....	....
20. Terraced dynamics	....	....
21. Numerous gradations of dynamics exploited	....	....

Study Guide 25

Items preceded by an asterisk (*) *are for use with the Regular Version only.*

CHAPTER R73/S57

I. Check (✔) those statements that are true with respect to music of the rococo period (1725-1775):

1. .... Originated in France
2. .... Inclined toward elegance; miniaturism
3. .... Inclined toward the monumental and grandoise
4. .... Identified as the *style galant*
*5. .... Primary goal: to charm, delight and entertain
*6. .... The harpsichord was the most popular keyboard instrument
* 7. .... Binary form predominates
*8. .... Dance rhythms avoided
*9. .... Ample use of ornamentation
*10. .... Homophonic texture stressed
*11. .... Contrapuntal texture stressed

CHAPTER R74/S57

II. Check (✔) those statements that are true with respect to pre-classical opera:

*1. .... Opera seria continued to be the favored type of opera throughout the eighteenth century.
*2. .... There was a discernible trend toward opera buffa (comic opera).
3. .... In contradistinction to baroque operatic practice, Gluck's reforms involved a greater fusion of musical and dramatic elements.
4. .... The bulk of Gluck's operas are based on contemporary themes.

III. Complete the following:

1. From the diverse developments of rococo music emerged a new idiom: the classical ....
*2. The new symphonic style of the Rococo was enriched with elements drawn from the operatic .... and ....
3. The rococo composer whose sonata style had a powerful influence upon Haydn, Mozart, and Beethoven was ....

BAROQUE TYPES

1. Overture
2. Recitativo: accompagnato, secco
3. Aria

4. Fugue
5. Concerto Grosso
6. Passacaglia

AURAL ANALYSIS

Handel: MESSIAH —Selections

Check (✔) the correct completions or associations:

I. No. 1, *Overture*

a) The first section is characterized by:

.... slow tempo   .... fast tempo

.... dotted rhythm   .... homophonic texture

b) The second section is characterized by:

.... slow tempo   .... fast tempo

.... fugal character   .... contrapuntal texture

c) The closing passage is characterized by:

.... slow tempo   .... fast tempo

.... homophonic texture   .... contrapuntal texture

d) The sequence of tempos is: .... fast-slow-fast   .... slow-fast-slow

e) This is a .... French overture   .... Italian overture

II. No. 14, *There were shepherds abiding in the field*

.... recitativo accompagnato   .... recitativo secco

And lo! the angel of the Lord came upon them

.... recitativo accompagnato   .... recitativo secco

No. 15, *And the angel said unto them, fear not*

.... recitativo accompagnato   .... recitativo secco

No. 16, *And suddenly there was with the angel a multitude of the heavenly host*

.... recitativo accompagnato   .... recitativo secco

No. 17, *Glory to God*

a) .... aria   .... chorus

b) Texture: .... exclusively homophonic

.... exclusively contrapuntal

.... duality of texture: homophonic and contrapuntal

III. No. 23, *He was despised*

1. .... recitative   .... aria

2. Character of first section: .... lyric   .... dramatic

3. Character of second section: .... lyric   .... dramatic

4. First section returns: .... yes   .... no

5. This is an .... aria da capo   .... aria without da capo

LISTENING GUIDE
Fugue

Handel: MESSIAH — No. 53, *Amen*

Exposition   1. *Subject* (tonic) — basses (vocal and instrumental)

                    A - - - men, A - - - - men, A - - - men,

         2. *Answer* (dominant) — tenors

         3. *Subject* (tonic) — altos

         4. *Answer* (dominant) — sopranos

          5. End of Exposition

Extension   6. a) *Subject* — violins I

             b) *Answer* — violins II

         7. *Subject* — tutti (theme in bass)

         8. Short *episode* (violins I; II)

         9. *Answer* — tutti (theme in bass)

Working out   10. First *stretto* section (canonic imitation)
section

        11. Expansion

        12. Second *stretto* section

            a) inversion

            b) original pattern

            c) inversion

Coda   13. a) *Pedal point*

             b) Grand pause   } (Trumpets and timpani prominent)

             c) Adagio; final cadence

After listening to this movement,

complete the Stylistic Evaluation Outline (Baroque), p. 101.

AURAL ANALYSES
Concerto Grosso

Bach: *Brandenburg Concerto* No. 2 in F Major — First Movement

Or other of your choice.   Check (✔)

1. Opening statement of movement proper is made by:

.... concertino alone

.... tutti (*ripieno*)

.... concertino and tutti

2. Concertante principle evident in interplay involving:

.... concertino and tutti

.... members of concertino only

.... individual soloists and tutti

3. Concertino and tutti join forces occasionally:

.... Yes   .... No

4. There is a theme that recurs (*ritornello*):

.... Yes   .... No

5. Levels of tonal volume result mainly from alternations of concertino and tutti:

.... Yes   .... No

6. There is an extended solo passage for a single instrument:

.... Yes   .... No

After listening to this movement,

complete the Stylistic Evaluation Outline (Baroque), p. 102.

Passacaglia

Bach: PASSACAGLIA AND FUGUE IN C MINOR

1. The theme of this Passacaglia is introduced in the

.... bass   .... treble

2. The theme of this Passacaglia is

.... continuously repeated or implied   .... stated only occasionally

3. A passacaglia is characterized by

.... continuous development of the thematic material   .... a series of variations

4. This Fugue contains

.... the theme of the Passacaglia   .... no reference to the Passacaglia theme

NAME .... CLASS .... DATE ....

STYLISTIC EVALUATION
Baroque

Composition .... Composer ....

1. Check (✔) the attributes that are prominently displayed in this composition:

.... Basso continuo (bass line in continuous motion)

.... Basso ostinato

.... Continuous melodic expansion

.... Terraced dynamics

.... Persistent rhythmic drive

.... Single mood ("affection") per movement

.... The harpsichord a basic member of the orchestra

.... Contrapuntal texture predominates

.... Homophonic texture predominates

.... Duality of textures; contrapuntal and homophonic

.... Virtuosity a prominent factor

.... Lyricism a prominent factor

.... Embellishments abundantly present

.... Vocal music: frequent repetition of words and phrases

.... Vocal music: word-tone painting

2. With respect to this period, list other stylistic attributes that may be present in this composition:

....

....

....

101

STYLISTIC EVALUATION
Baroque

Composition .... Composer ....

1. Check (✔) the attributes that are prominently displayed in this composition:

.... Basso continuo (bass line in continuous motion)

.... Basso ostinato

.... Continuous melodic expansion

.... Terraced dynamics

.... Persistent rhythmic drive

.... Single mood ("affection") per movement

.... The harpsichord a basic member of the orchestra

.... Contrapuntal texture predominates

.... Homophonic texture predominates

.... Duality of textures; contrapuntal and homophonic

.... Virtuosity a prominent factor

.... Lyricism a prominent factor

.... Embellishments abundantly present

.... Vocal music: frequent repetition of words and phrases

.... Vocal music: word-tone painting

2. With respect to this period, list other stylistic attributes that may be present in this composition:

....

....

....

General Review V. Medieval, Renaissance, and Baroque Music

Match each item in Column II to its appropriate association in Column I:

I. *Periods in Music History*

	COLUMN I	COLUMN II
1.	850-1150: the period that saw the rise of polyphony	Baroque
2.	1150-1450: the period in which learned musicians mastered the art of constructing extended musical works	Gothic
3.	1450-1600: the period that was influenced by the rediscovered cultures of ancient Greece and Rome	Renaissance
4.	1600-1750: the period in which opera originated and instrumental music achieved comparable importance to vocal music	Rococo
5.	1725-1755: the period in which the *style galant* was current in music	Romanesque

II. *Musical Textures*

	COLUMN I	COLUMN II
1.	The simplest kind of texture: single-voiced music	Homophony
2.	A texture resulting from the combination of two or more voices	Monophony
3.	A texture comprised of a melody and a supporting harmonic background	Polyphony

(General Review V continued on pages 104, 105, 106.)

III. *Compositional Types and Devices*

COLUMN I   COLUMN II

1. .... The art of combining two or more musical lines, each with a rhythmic life of its own   A Cappella

2. .... The strictest type of imitation, in which the whole length of a musical line is restated in another voice   Agnus Dei

3. .... The great heritage of monophonic music identified with the Catholic liturgy   Canon

    Cantus Firmus

4. ....

  ....   Concerto Grosso

  ....   Counterpoint

  .... The five sections of the Mass that are most commonly set to music   Credo

  ....   Da Capo Aria

  ....   Gloria

    Gregorian Chant

    Klavier

5. .... The Latin term meaning *fixed melody*   Kyrie

    Madrigal
    Motet

6. .... The Mass for the Dead   Opera

    Opera Seria

7. .... A term that denotes a choral work without instrumental accompaniment   Oratorio
    Cantata

8. ....

  .... Apart from the Mass, the two most representative types of Renaissance vocal music   Requiem

    Ritornello

    Sanctus

9. .... A musical refrain that returns throughout a work   Sonata da Camera
    Sonata da Chiesa

10. .... A musical-dramatic form that emerged in 1600

11. .... The word used in Germany as the general term for a keyboard instrument

12. .... The baroque formal or serious opera

13. .... The operatic component that was influential in establishing ternary form as a basic formula of musical structure

14. ....

  .... Two important compositional types that came out of a fusion of sixteenth-century vocal polyphony and baroque opera

15. ....

  .... The two established types of baroque trio sonata

16. .... A type of composition that features a small group of instruments versus a larger group

NAME .... CLASS .... DATE ....

COLUMN I	COLUMN II

17. .... The small group of instruments in the concerto grosso

18. .... The large group of instruments in the concerto grosso

19. .... An instrumental work consisting of several contrasting dance movements, all in the same key

20. .... A contrapuntal composition, based on the principle of imitation, in which the theme, treated as subject and answer, dominates the composition

21. .... The first section of a fugue, in which the theme is introduced in each voice

22. .... A quasi-fugal passage in a nonfugal piece

23. .... A composition in stately tempo and triple meter, utilizing the principle of the ground bass

24. .... An instrumental form relating to the passacaglia but based on a succession of harmonies repeated throughout the composition

25. .... A German Protestant hymn

26. .... A musical setting of that portion of the Gospels dealing with the suffering and death of Christ

27. .... A baroque keyboard piece whose form is free and whose character is rhapsodic and virtuosic

28. .... A type of overture in one movement generally patterned in a slow-fast (fugal)-slow sequence

29. .... A type of overture in one movement generally patterned in a fast-slow-fast sequence, containing no fugal section

30. .... The pre-classical type of light, comic opera

COLUMN II

Chaconne
Chorale
Concertino
Exposition
French Overture
Fugato
Fugue
Italian Overture
Opera Buffa
Passacaglia
Passion
Suite
Toccata
Tutti

IV. *Baroque Musical Practice*

	COLUMN I	COLUMN II

1. .... The early seventeenth-century operatic style

2. ....
.... } Three designations for a system involving the "realization" of a bass line
....

3. .... } Two designations for a short musical phrase persistently repeated in the bass while the upper
.... parts pursue a variety of musical changes

4. .... } The modes that replaced the Church modes as the chief basis for melodic and harmonic struc-
.... ture in Western music

5. .... An adjustment in tuning that divides the octave into twelve equal intervals

6. .... A common practice involving word-tone painting in vocal music and the prevalence of a single mood per movement in instrumental music

7. .... The element of music manifesting a dynamic unflagging drive

8. .... The principle of continuous melodic expansion

9. .... A characteristic feature pertaining to two alternating levels of tonal volume

10. .... A manifestation pertaining to a high degree of skill in performance

11. .... Extemporization as an integral factor in performance

12. ....
.... } The major keyboard instruments
....

COLUMN II

Basso Continuo

Basso Ostinato

Clavichord, Harpsichord, and Organ

Continuous Melody

Doctrine of the Affections

Equal Temperament

Figured Bass

Ground Bass

Improvisation

Major

Minor

Rhythm

Stile Rappresentativo (Representational Style)

Terraced Dynamics

Thorough Bass

Virtuosity

Part Six

THE TWENTIETH CENTURY

Study Guide 25

CHAPTERS R75/S58, R78/S60

Complete the following:

1. The postromantic period extended from around .... *1890* .... to ..... *1910* ....

2. The country in which the impressionistic movement originated was .... *France* ....,...........

3. The term "impressionism" in art originated with Claude Monet's painting titled .... *Impression* .... *Sun Rising* .... (1867).

4. Impressionism in music was greatly influenced by the impressionistic movement in ..... *art: painting* .... and the symbolist movement in .... *poetry* ....

5. With impressionistic harmony, it is not a matter of consonance versus dissonance but of relative degrees of .... *dissonance* ....

6. The composer who dominated musical impressionism was ...... *Debussy* ....

CHAPTERS R78/S60, R79/S61

Check (✔) those statements that describe tendencies apparent in musical impressionism:

1. .... Use of medieval modes; exotic and novel scales (including the whole tone scale)
2. .... A propensity for primary intervals in chord structure (octaves, fourths, fifths) .
3. .... Use of dissonance as a value in itself
4. .... Use of chords in parallel motion
5. .... Strict adherence to traditional harmonic procedures
6. .... Use of new tone combinations including the ninth chord
7. .... A trend toward the disintegration of the major-minor system
8. .... Veiled blending of orchestral colors
9. .... A treatment of rhythm that tends to minimize the regularity of accent on the first beat of a measure
10. .... Inclination toward the miniature — short lyric pieces
11. .... Predilection for program music, tone painting, nature worship
12. .... Addiction to lyricism
13. .... Desire to unite music, painting, poetry
14. .... The sonata-allegro is the preferred form
15. ....✗....... Orchestration in which the timbre of individual instruments stands out against the mass
16. .... Disinterest in piano music, chamber music, and songs

ROMANTICISM vs. IMPRESSIONISM

Check (✔) *either or both* of the periods in Column II to indicate those characteristics or practices in Column I that are prominent in romantic and impressionistic music:

COLUMN I	COLUMN II	
	ROMANTICISM	IMPRESSIONISM
1. Significant use of whole tone and exotic scales	....	X
2. The heroic and the grandoise	X	....
3. Interest in nature subjects	X	X
4. Lyricism	X	X
5. Union of the arts — music, painting, and poetry	X	X
6. The symphony as a major means of expression	X	X
7. Pictorialism; musical descriptiveness	X	X
8. The short (piano) piece and art song	X	X

In light of the evidence presented by the completion of the above chart, check (✔) the statement below that represents a valid conclusion:

.... Romanticism and impressionism are two totally opposed stylistic periods.

X Romanticism and impressionism are stylistic periods that exhibit many common qualities.

Notes

AURAL ANALYSIS
Postromanticism vs. Impressionism

The postromantic era was one of transition. In point of time, it encompasses impressionism. The music that is called postromantic represents a basic adherence to and extension of the nineteenth-century romantic esthetic; that which is called impressionistic, while retaining similarities to romanticism, manifests unique and striking departures.

Strauss:
DON JUAN, Opus 20
Or others of your choice.

Debussy:
PRÉLUDE À L'APRÈS-MIDI D'UN FAUNE

Composer ....   Composer ....
Composition ....   Composition ....

Listen to these two works and concentrate on the manner in which the composer uses the materials of music.

1. In the area of orchestral music, the impressionists treated orchestration as a predominant factor in composition. With respect to *timbre*, describe the qualities that distinguish these two pieces.

   ....

   ....

2. With respect to the other elements of music, indicate — with a word or phrase — what you hear in these works, noting similarities and differences.

   Melody ....
   Harmony ....
   Rhythm ....
   Tempo ....
   Dynamics ....
   Pitch ....
   Form ....

3. In the light of your analysis, check (✔) the appropriate statement below:

   a) .... Postromanticism and impressionism are two totally opposed stylistic periods.

   b) .... Postromanticism and impressionism are stylistic periods that exhibit many common qualities.

AURAL ANALYSIS
Postromanticism vs. Impressionism

Composer ....   Composer ....

Composition ....   Composition ....

1. In the area of orchestral music, the impressionists treated orchestration as a predominant factor in composition. With respect to *timbre*, describe the qualities that distinguish these two pieces.

   ....

   ....

   ....

2. With respect to the other elements of music, indicate — with a word or phrase — what you hear in these works, noting similarities and differences.

   Melody ....

   Harmony ....

   Rhythm ....

   Tempo ....

   Dynamics ....

   Pitch ....

   Form ....

3. In the light of your analysis, check (✔) the appropriate statement below:

   a) .... Postromanticism and impressionism are two totally opposed stylistic periods.

   b) .... Postromanticism and impressionism are stylistic periods that exhibit many common qualities.

NAME ....   CLASS ....   DATE ....

Study Guide 26

CHAPTER R82/S63

I. With respect to currents in twentieth-century music, match each of the following items to its appropriate association:

Expressionism   Machine Music   New Classicism

New Nationalism   Non-Western Cultures

1. N.W.C. ....   Sources of rhythmic treatment inspired by the music of Africa and Asia

2. M.M. ....   The glorification of industrial equipment

3. N.C. ....   The reaffirmation of eighteenth-century esthetic principles

4. N.N. ....   A deepened interest in native folk elements

5. E ....   A hyperexpressive musical language that aspired to overwhelming effect and intensity

II. Check (✔) the statements that are true with respect to currents in twentieth-century music:

1. ....X.... There was a reaction against some of the esthetic values of romanticism.

2. ....X.... Ballet continued as an important art form.

3. .... Neoclassicism was directed toward an exact duplication of baroque music.

4. .... The new nationalism contributed to the uncovering of harsh dissonances, irregular rhythmic patterns, and archaic modes.

5. ....X.... The irrational, the macabre, the grotesque and the distorted found uninhibited exposure in German expressionism.

*6. ....X.... Expressionistic music favored an ultra-dissonant harmonic language, wide leaps in the melody, the use of instruments in their extreme registers and the rejection of tonality. (p. R479)

Characteristics of nineteenth- and twentieth-century music

CHAPTER R83/S64

Check (✔) the appropriate column to indicate the relevant reference for each statement:

IN 19TH-CENTURY MUSIC	IN 20TH-CENTURY MUSIC	
1. X		Standard metric patterns prevail.
	X	Use of nonsymmetrical metric patterns.
2.	X	Frequent shifts in the metrical flow within a movement.
X		A single meter prevails through an entire movement.
3.	X	Rhythm manifests an unprecedented degree of freedom and flexibility.
X		Rhythm is based on the regular recurrence of accent.
4. X		Melody is predominantly based on balanced phrases.
	X	Melody is frequently asymmetrical in structure.
5.	X	Melody is based primarily on an instrumental conception.
X		Melody is fundamentally vocal in character.
6.	X	Harmony often includes chords based on the interval of the fourth.
X		Chord structures are based predominantly on the interval of the third.
7. X		Consonance is treated as the harmonic norm and dissonance as a temporary disturbance of the norm.
	X	The difference between consonance and dissonance becomes a difference in the degree of dissonance.
8. X		The emphasis is on homophonic texture.
	X	The emphasis is on contrapuntal texture.
9.	X	An inclination toward a small orchestra and a lean sound.
X		A preference for a large orchestra and brilliant, rich sonorities.
10. X		Instrumental color is frequently used for its own sake.
	X	Instrumental color is used to bring out the lines of counterpoint and outline the form.
11. X		The piano is used predominantly in a solo capacity.
	X	The piano is accorded a place in the orchestral ensemble, where its percussive capacity is exploited.
12. X		America contributed nothing unique or outstanding to art music.
	X	The influence of American jazz is evident in art music.

Study Guide 27

CHAPTER R84/S65

I. Complete the following:

1. New conceptions of tonality that emerged in the twentieth century generally followed one of three paths:

   a) *expanded tonality*

   b) *polytonality*

   c) *atonality*

2. In the major-minor system, the number of different tones that constitute a key is *7*.

3. The expanded scheme of tonality that emerged in the twentieth century involved the free use of *12* chromatic tones around a center.

4. Tonality implies the supremacy of a single *key* and a single *tonal* center.

5. Presenting two or more keys simultaneously is called *polytonality*.

6. The rejection of the principle of key is called *atonality*.

7. A composer who pioneered in atonal music was *Schoenberg*.

8. In excluding consonance, atonal music moves within varying levels of *dissonance*.

9. According to Schoenberg's twelve-tone method, every composition is based on an arbitrary arrangement of twelve chromatic tones called a *tone row* or *basic set*.

10. Schoenberg's method of composing with twelve tones is referred to by three designations:

    a) *serial tech*   b) *dodecaphonic*   c) *twelve-tone*.

II. Check (✔) the statements that are true with respect to Schoenberg's method of twelve-tone composition:

1. ...✔... In the tone row none of the tones may be repeated except by immediate succession.
2. .... When the basic set has been presented it is repeated throughout the work with the twelve tones always in the same order.
3. ...✔... The row may undergo inversion, retrograde, and retrograde of the inversion.
4. ...✔... The original row and its variants may begin on any one of the twelve chromatic tones.
5. .... The tones of a twelve-tone row are arranged in order of importance with the central tone as its tonic.
6. ...✔... The basic set is the unifying idea that engenders all the other ideas within a composition.
7. .... The tone row never appears within a chord, therefore, harmony is not an essential factor in Schoenberg's scheme.
8. .... Twelve-tone music seeks the utmost variety without regard for unity.
9. ...✔... Dodecaphonic melody tends towards enormous leaps and a jagged line.
10. ...✔... Twelve-tone music is essentially contrapuntal in texture.
11. .... The twelve-tone method is strongly supported by sequences, balanced phrases, and cadences.
12. ...✔... The twelve-tone method embodies Schoenberg's doctrine of "perpetual variation".
13. ...✔... Complex manipulations of a tone row eventually tend to obliterate the aural recognition of its original formulation.
14. ...✔... In dodecaphonic music, logic predominates within a rigidly organized system.
15. ...✔... The 1950s and 1960s saw the eclipse of dodecaphonic music.

Study Guide 28

CHAPTER R85/s66

I. Check (✔) the statements that are true with respect to Stravinsky:

1. .... His career is characterized by continuous development through periods of experimentation and stylistic change.

2. .... He was a leader in the revitalization of rhythm in Western music.

3. .... He found the medium of ballet unsuited to his artistic expression.

4. .... His music is all atonal.

5. .... He is one of the great orchestrators of our time.

6. .... He has shown a strong inclination toward neoclassicism.

7. .... In his late years he wrote twelve-tone music.

CHAPTER R86/s67

II. Check (✔) the statements that are true with respect to Bartók:

1. .... His objective was to reconcile the folk melody of his native Hungary with the main currents of European music.

2. .... He found sources for melody and harmony outside the scope of the major-minor system.

3. .... Classic and romantic elements intermingle in his work.

4. .... His harmony excludes dissonance.

5. .... His involvement with atonality did not cause him to abandon the principle of key.

6. .... Meter changes within a single composition are extremely rare.

7. .... Like Stravinsky, he played a major role in the revitalization of rhythm in Western music.

8. .... He was as untraditional in respect to form as he was to melody, harmony, and rhythm.

9. .... He is considered one of the masters of modern piano writing.

10. .... In accordance with the twentieth-century tendency, he frequently makes use of the piano as an instrument of percussion and rhythm.

11. .... His music encompasses the diverse trends of the twentieth century, including polytonality, atonality, expressionism, neoclassicism, and nationalism.

III. Check (✔) the statements that are true with respect to Schoenberg:

1. .... His method of composition moved toward a rejection of tonality — an atonal idiom.

2. .... The spirit of romanticism was alien to Schoenberg's early esthetic ideals.

3. .... In his atonal-expressionist music, the distinction between consonance and dissonance as well as the sense of home key are abolished.

4. .... In *Pierrot Lunaire*, he introduced an eerily expressive kind of declamation called *sprechstimme*.

5. .... In his later works, tonal and atonal elements coexist with the twelve-tone style.

Notes

AURAL ANALYSIS
Stylistic Evaluation (Twentieth Century)

Stravinsky: *PETRUSHKA* (First Tableau)

Or another of your choice.

The music of the twentieth century involves a diversity of trends manifesting radical departures from traditional concepts as well as adherence to principles and devices of the past. To exemplify these trends, several contrasting compositions should be chosen for style analysis. The following evaluation outline lists attributes of the twentieth century and of former periods.

Instructions:

1. Familiarize yourself with the evaluation outline.

2. Listen to the composition for general impression.

3. Listen again and complete the outline. Entries may be made during the listening process.

Composer ....   Composition ....

Check (✔) the attributes that are prominently displayed in this composition with respect to the stylistic elements in each of the following categories:

NEW ELEMENTS OF STYLE

.... Melody of an unlyric nature

.... Harmony predominantly dissonant

.... Rhythm a dominating factor; frequent changes of meter

.... Prominence of percussiveness

.... Electronically generated sound

.... Serial technique

.... Jazz influence

.... Others: ....

PREROMANTIC ELEMENTS OF STYLE

.... Rhythm: regular meters predominate

.... Contrapuntal texture prominent

.... Orchestra: limited variety of timbre

.... Sonority: tends toward a light, sparse sound

.... Tempo: fairly constant within a movement

.... Others: ....

ROMANTIC ELEMENTS OF STYLE

.... Melody of a lyric nature

.... Harmony: resolution of dissonance stressed

.... Orchestra: wide variety of timbre

.... Sonority: tends toward a rich, colorful sound

.... Tempo: fluctuates conspicuously within a movement

.... Others: ....

In the light of your analysis, this composition incorporates elements of the following styles: Check (✔)

.... New   .... Preromantic   .... Romantic

AURAL ANALYSIS
Stylistic Evaluation (Twentieth Century)

Bartók: *CONCERTO FOR ORCHESTRA* (First movement)
Or another of your choice.

Composer .... Composition ....

Check (✔) the attributes that are prominently displayed in this composition with respect to the stylistic elements in each of the following categories:

NEW ELEMENTS OF STYLE

.... Melody of an unlyric nature

.... Harmony predominantly dissonant

.... Rhythm a dominating factor; frequent changes of meter

.... Prominence of percussiveness

.... Electronically generated sound

.... Serial technique

.... Jazz influence

.... Others: ....

PREROMANTIC ELEMENTS OF STYLE

.... Rhythm: regular meters predominate

.... Contrapuntal texture prominent

.... Orchestra: limited variety of timbre

.... Sonority: tends toward a light, sparse sound

.... Tempo: fairly constant within a movement

.... Others: ....

ROMANTIC ELEMENTS OF STYLE

.... Melody of a lyric nature

.... Harmony: resolution of dissonance stressed

.... Orchestra: wide variety of timbre

.... Sonority: tends toward a rich, colorful sound

.... Tempo: fluctuates conspicuously within a movement

.... Others: ....

In the light of your analysis, this composition incorporates elements of the following styles: Check (✔)

.... New   .... Preromantic   .... Romantic

Study Guide 29

Items preceded by an asterisk (*) are for use with the Regular Version only.

CHAPTER R88/s69

Check (✔) the statements that are true with respect to Berg:

1. .... He effected an individually expressive style within the Schoenbergian twelve-tone technique.

*2. .... With the opera *Wozzeck*, he achieved international fame.

3. .... All romantic inclinations disappeared from his music once he embraced the dodecaphonic style.

*4. .... Like Schoenberg, he leaned toward the formal structures of the past.

*5. .... His later works reveal tendencies toward musical expressionism.

*6. .... He differed from Schoenberg in that he never abandoned key signatures.

*7. .... He is one of the most widely admired masters of the twelve-tone school.

8. .... The opera *Wozzeck* encompasses such varied elements as atonal-expressionism, twelve-tone procedures, tonal pasages, and the use of leitmotifs.

CHAPTER R89/s69

Check (✔) the statements that are true with respect to Webern:

*1. .... Along with Berg, he was a disciple of Schoenberg.

2. .... Of Schoenberg's followers, he was the one who most strongly upheld the principle of tonality.

3. .... His works reveal a strong inclination toward brevity.

4. .... His music is consistently scored for traditional instrumental combinations restricted to their middle registers.

5. .... Each tone in his overall scheme is assigned a specific function, conferring upon the individual sound an unprecedented importance.

*6. .... He extended the serial process to include timbre and rhythm as well as pitch.

*7. .... He is the dominant influence in dodecaphonic thinking in the mid-twentieth century.

AURAL ANALYSIS
Stylistic Evaluation (Twentieth Century)

Schoenberg: *FIVE PIECES FOR ORCHESTRA*, OPUS 16

Or another of your choice:

Composer .... Composition ....

Check (✔) the attributes that are prominently displayed in this composition with respect to the **stylistic elements** in each of the following categories:

NEW ELEMENTS OF STYLE

.... Melody of an unlyric nature

.... Harmony predominantly dissonant

.... Rhythm a dominating factor; frequent changes of meter

.... Prominence of percussiveness

.... Electronically generated sound

.... Serial technique

.... Jazz influence

.... Others: ....

PREROMANTIC ELEMENTS OF STYLE

.... Rhythm: regular meters predominate

.... Contrapuntal texture prominent

.... Orchestra: limited variety of timbre

.... Sonority: tends toward a light, sparse sound

.... Tempo: fairly constant within a movement

.... Others: ....

ROMANTIC ELEMENTS OF STYLE

.... Melody of a lyric nature

.... Harmony: resolution of dissonance stressed

.... Orchestra: wide variety of timbre

.... Sonority: tends toward a rich, colorful sound

.... Tempo: fluctuates conspicuously within a movement

.... Others: ....

In the light of your analysis, this composition incorporates elements of the following styles: Check (✔)

.... New   .... Preromantic   .... Romantic

AURAL ANALYSIS
Stylistic Evaluation (Twentieth Century)

Webern: *FIVE PIECES FOR ORCHESTRA*, OPUS 10

Or another of your choice:

Composer .... Composition ....

Check (✔) the attributes that are prominently displayed in this composition with respect to the stylistic elements in each of the following categories:

NEW ELEMENTS OF STYLE

.... Melody of an unlyric nature

.... Harmony predominantly dissonant

.... Rhythm a dominating factor; frequent changes of meter

.... Prominence of percussiveness

.... Electronically generated sound

.... Serial technique

.... Jazz influence

.... Others: ....

PREROMANTIC ELEMENTS OF STYLE

.... Rhythm: regular meters predominate

.... Contrapuntal texture prominent

.... Orchestra: limited variety of timbre

.... Sonority: tends toward a light, sparse sound

.... Tempo: fairly constant within a movement

.... Others: ....

ROMANTIC ELEMENTS OF STYLE

.... Melody of a lyric nature

.... Harmony: resolution of dissonance stressed

.... Orchestra: wide variety of timbre

.... Sonority: tends toward a rich, colorful sound

.... Tempo: fluctuates conspicuously within a movement

.... Others: ....

In the light of your analysis, this composition incorporates elements of the following styles: Check (✔)

.... New .... Preromantic .... Romantic

AURAL ANALYSIS
Stylistic Evaluation (Twentieth Century)

Composer .... Composition ....

Check ($\checkmark$) the attributes that are prominently displayed in this composition with respect to the stylistic elements in each of the following categories:

NEW ELEMENTS OF STYLE

.... Melody of an unlyric nature

.... Harmony predominantly dissonant

.... Rhythm a dominating factor; frequent changes of meter

.... Prominence of percussiveness

.... Electronically generated sound

.... Serial technique

.... Jazz influence

Others: ....

PREROMANTIC ELEMENTS OF STYLE

.... Rhythm: regular meters predominate

.... Contrapuntal texture prominent

.... Orchestra: limited variety of timbre

.... Sonority: tends toward a light, sparse sound

.... Tempo: fairly constant within a movement

Others: ....

ROMANTIC ELEMENTS OF STYLE

.... Melody of a lyric nature

.... Harmony: resolution of dissonance stressed

.... Orchestra: wide variety of timbre

.... Sonority: tends toward a rich, colorful sound

.... Tempo: fluctuates conspicuously within a movement

Others: ....

In the light of your analysis, this composition incorporates elements of the following styles: Check ($\checkmark$)

.... New   .... Preromantic   .... Romantic

NAME .... CLASS .... DATE ....

Study Guide 30

CHAPTERS R27, 77, 80, 81, 90/S59, 62, 69

Match each composer in the following list with the appropriate statement:

Bloch	Britten	Delius	Elgar
Falla	Fauré	Hindemith	Honegger
Khatchaturian	Kodály	Krenek	Mahler
Milhaud	Orff	Poulenc	Prokofiev
Rachmaninov	Ravel	Scriabin	Shostakovich
Strauss	Vaughan Williams	Walton	Weill

1. .... A German composer of a series of renowned symphonic poems
(1864-1949)

2. .... A Bohemian [whose music expresses the postromantic spirit] and who
(1860-1911) achieved fame in Vienna as composer and conductor

3. .... A postimpressionist whose music displays classicist tendencies
(1875-1937)

4. .... A French composer best known for his Requiem (1887)
(1845-1924)

5. .... A Russian famous for his grandiose symphonic poems
(1872-1915)

6. .... Famous for his piano concertos and the *Rhapsody on a Theme by Paganini*
(1873-1943)

7. .... The English composer of the *Enigma Variations*
(1857-1934)

8. .... His choral work *Sea Drift* is based on the poem by Walt Whitman
(1862-1934)

9. .... Regarded by the British as one of their foremost musicians
(1872-1958)

10. .... The leading French figure in contemporary music after the death of Ravel
(1892-   )

11. .... A French composer whose interest in "machine music" resulted in *Pacific
(1892-1955) 231*

12. .... One of the outstanding French song composers of our time
(1899-1963)

13. .... Two of his most popular compositions are the *Classical Symphony* and
(1891-1953) *Peter and the Wolf*

14. .... At nineteen, his First Symphony brought him instant international success
(1906-   )

15. .... A Russian composer whose piano concerto (1936) combines Armenian
(1903-   ) folk elements with the grand virtuoso tradition of Liszt

123

16. *Hindemith*
(1895-1963)
A German who based his harmonies on the free use of twelve tones without abandoning tonality

17. *Kodaly*
(1882-1967)
Associated with Béla Bartók in the collection and study of Hungarian [and Rumanian] folk music

18. *Orff*
(1895-   )
His "dramatic cantata" *Carmina burana* is based on thirteenth-century songs and poems

19. *Krenek*
(1900-   )
His book *Music Here and Now* (1939) probes the complexities of contemporary musical thought

20. *Weill*
(1900-1950)
Through repeated revivals his *The Three-Penny Opera* has achieved international fame

21. *Falla*
(1876-1946)
The culminating figure of the Spanish movement to create a national art based on authentic folklore

22. *Bloch*
(1880-1959)
A Swiss-American composer whose works show a strong identification with Hebraic themes

23. *Walton*
(1902-   )
A composer whose choral style reflects the heritage of the rich English choral tradition

24. *Britten*
(1913-   )
An English composer whose works affirm his position as one of the foremost operatic composers of our time

Notes

General Review VI. The Twentieth Century

Match each item in the following list to its appropriate association:

Atonality	Contrapuntal Polyphony	Expressionism	Harmony
Impressionism	Jazz	Major-Minor	Melody
New Classicism	New Nationalism	Non-Western Cultures	Piano
Polytonality	Rhythm	Serial Technique	Timbre	Tone Row

1. .... A stylistic period, at the turn of the twentieth century, that abandoned the grandiose rhetoric of romanticism in favor of vagueness, tonal ambiguity, and an increased preoccupation with color

2. .... The two modes that lost their dominant hold on music with the inception of impressionism

3. .... Sources of rhythmic treatment inspired by the music of Africa and Asia

4. .... The reaffirmation of eighteenth-century esthetic principles

5. .... A deepened interest in native folk elements

6. .... A hyperexpressive musical language that aspired to overwhelming effect and intensity

7. .... The element of music that involved frequent changes of meter within a piece or movement

8. .... The element of music that is now based primarily on an instrumental rather than a vocal conception

9. .... The element of music characterized by the prevalence of dissonance

10. .... The type of texture that receives emphasis in twentieth-century music

11. .... The element of music used to bring out the lines of counterpoint and outline the form

12. .... A keyboard instrument that gains acceptance as an integral member of the orchestra

13. .... A distinctly American musical genre, which had a significant influence upon twentieth-century art music

14. .... The use of two or more keys simultaneously

15. .... The rejection of the principle of key

16. .... A method of composition with twelve tones, originated by Schoenberg

17. .... An arbitrary arrangement of the twelve chromatic pitches that serve as the basic set in a dodecaphonic composition

AURAL ANALYSIS
Stylistic Evaluation (Twentieth Century)

Composer .... Composition ....

Check (✔) the attributes that are prominently displayed in this composition with respect to the stylistic elements in each of the following categories:

NEW ELEMENTS OF STYLE

.... Melody of an unlyric nature

.... Harmony predominantly dissonant

.... Rhythm a dominating factor; frequent changes of meter

.... Prominence of percussiveness

.... Electronically generated sound

.... Serial technique

.... Jazz influence

.... Others: ....

PREROMANTIC ELEMENTS OF STYLE

.... Rhythm: regular meters predominate

.... Contrapuntal texture prominent

.... Orchestra: limited variety of timbre

.... Sonority: tends toward a light, sparse sound

.... Tempo: fairly constant within a movement

.... Others: ....

ROMANTIC ELEMENTS OF STYLE

.... Melody of a lyric nature

.... Harmony: resolution of dissonance stressed

.... Orchestra: wide variety of timbre

.... Sonority: tends toward a rich, colorful sound

.... Tempo: fluctuates conspicuously within a movement

.... Others: ....

In the light of your analysis, this composition incorporates elements of the following styles: Check (✔)

.... New   .... Preromantic   .... Romantic

Part Seven

THE AMERICAN SCENE

Study Guide 31

Items preceded by an asterisk (*) are for use with the Regular Version only.

CHAPTER R92/S71

Complete the following statements (for True-False statements, circle T or F):

*1. T F   The early twentieth century saw the emergence of a strong native American school of composition.

*2.   From the 1920s on, the growth and development of American composers were aided by:

a) ....   d) ....

b) ....   e) ....

c) ....

*3. T F   The decade before the Second World War saw the United States emerge as the musical center of the world.

4.   American composers who aspired to give expression to the life about them derived ample raw material from the following sources:

a) ....   e) ....

b) ....   f) ....

c) ....   g) ....

d) ....

5. T F   Since the 1920s, every American composer has been inclined toward the use of folk elements and local color.

CHAPTER R93/p.S401   IVES (1874-1954)

Respond to the incomplete and True-False statements with respect to the designated composer.

1. T F   He is considered the first truly American composer of the twentieth century.

*2. T F   His career was devoted solely to music.

3.   Sources that inspired his tone imagery were:

....

....

....

4.   Advanced conceptions and procedures in which he pioneered were:

• ....

....

....

CHAPTER R94/p.S404   VARÈSE (1883-1965)

1. T F   His music is within the classic-romantic tradition.

*2. T F   He pioneered in the field of electronic music.

*3. T F   By the 1950s there existed a public receptive to his experimental music.

4. T F   His revolutionary music derives its inspiration from the metropolis and its industrial life.

5. T F   Much of his music is percussion-oriented, as in *Ionisation*.

6. T F   His concern was primarily with sonority and rhythm.

CHAPTER R94/p.S410   SESSIONS (1896-   )

1.   Responsive to the most significant currents of his time, Sessions's compositions show evidence of:

            a) ....

            b) ....

            c) ....

            d) ....

2.   The central place in his output is held by his eight ....

CHAPTER R94/p.S410   GERSHWIN (1898-1937)

1. T F   The jazz idiom was to him a natural form of musical expression.

2. T F   His determination to keep the "popular" and "classical" separate is evidenced in the *Rhapsody in Blue*.

3.   His masterpiece is an opera called ....

CHAPTER R95/p.S406   COPLAND (1900-   )

1. T F   He is generally recognized as the representative figure among contemporary American composers.

*2.   His compositions mirror some of the dominant trends of his time. Name three:

            a) ....

            b) ....

            c) ....

3.   His preoccupation with nationalism is evidenced by the titles of several of his compositions. Name three:

            a) ....

            b) ....

            c) ....

Study Guide 32

CHAPTER R95/S72

Match each composer in the following list with the appropriate statement:

Barber	Bernstein	Hanson	Harris
Menotti	Moore	Schuman	Thomson

1. .... An American who wrote the opera *Vanessa* on a libretto by Menotti
   (1910-   )

2. .... The composer of *The Ballad of Baby Doe* who regarded romanticism as a
   (1893-1969)   characteristic American trait

3. .... An American who came into prominence with his opera *Four Saints in*
   (1896-   )   *Three Acts* on a libretto by Gertrude Stein

4. .... A notable contributor to the repertory of American symphonies
   (1898-   )

5. .... A traditionalist made famous by his Second Symphony, the *Romantic*
   (1896-   )

6. .... A composer of instrumental music mainly in large forms, such as his Third
   (1910-   )   Symphony and *New England Triptych*

7. .... An Italian, educated in the United States, who had outstanding success with
   (1911-   )   his operas including *The Medium* and *Amahl and the Night Visitors*

8. .... The first American-born conductor of the New York Philharmonic Orchestra
   (1918-   )

AURAL ANALYSIS
Stylistic Evaluation (Twentieth Century)

Ives: *THREE PLACES IN NEW ENGLAND*
Or another of your choice.

Composer .... Composition ....

Check (✔) the attributes that are prominently displayed in this composition with respect to the stylistic elements in each of the following categories:

NEW ELEMENTS OF STYLE

.... Melody of an unlyric nature

.... Harmony predominantly dissonant

.... Rhythm a dominating factor; frequent changes of meter

.... Prominence of percussiveness

.... Electronically generated sound

.... Serial technique

.... Jazz influence

.... Others: ....

PREROMANTIC ELEMENTS OF STYLE

.... Rhythm: regular meters predominate

.... Contrapuntal texture prominent

.... Orchestra: limited variety of timbre

.... Sonority: tends toward a light, sparse sound

.... Tempo: fairly constant within a movement

.... Others: ....

ROMANTIC ELEMENTS OF STYLE

.... Melody of a lyric nature

.... Harmony: resolution of dissonance stressed

.... Orchestra: wide variety of timbre

.... Sonority: tends toward a rich, colorful sound

.... Tempo: fluctuates conspicuously within a movement

.... Others: ....

In the light of your analysis, this composition incorporates elements of the following styles: Check (✔)

.... New   .... Preromantic   .... Romantic

AURAL ANALYSIS
Stylistic Evaluation (Twentieth Century)

Copland: *BILLY THE KID*

Or another of your choice.

Instructions:

1. Familiarize yourself with the evaluation outline.

2. Listen to the composition for general impression.

3. Listen again and complete the outline. Entries may be made during the listening process.

Composer .... Composition ....

Check (✔) the attributes that are prominently displayed in this composition with respect to the stylistic elements in each of the following categories:

NEW ELEMENTS OF STYLE

.... Melody of an unlyric nature

.... Harmony predominantly dissonant

.... Rhythm a dominating factor; frequent changes of meter

.... Prominence of percussiveness

.... Electronically generated sound

.... Serial technique

.... Jazz influence

.... Others: ....

PREROMANTIC ELEMENTS OF STYLE

.... Rhythm: regular meters predominate

.... Contrapuntal texture prominent

.... Orchestra: limited variety of timbre

.... Sonority: tends toward a light, sparse sound

.... Tempo: fairly constant within a movement

.... Others: ....

ROMANTIC ELEMENTS OF STYLE

.... Melody of a lyric nature

.... Harmony: resolution of dissonance stressed

.... Orchestra: wide variety of timbre

.... Sonority: tends toward a rich, colorful sound

.... Tempo: fluctuates conspicuously within a movement

.... Others: ....

In the light of your analysis, this composition incorporates elements of the following styles: Check (✔)

.... New .... Preromantic .... Romantic

AURAL ANALYSIS
Stylistic Evaluation (Twentieth Century)

Composer .... Composition ....

Check (✔) the attributes that are prominently displayed in this composition with respect to the stylistic elements in each of the following categories:

NEW ELEMENTS OF STYLE

.... Melody of an unlyric nature

.... Harmony predominantly dissonant

.... Rhythm a dominating factor; frequent changes of meter

.... Prominence of percussiveness

.... Electronically generated sound

.... Serial technique

.... Jazz influence

Others: ....

PREROMANTIC ELEMENTS OF STYLE

.... Rhythm: regular meters predominate

.... Contrapuntal texture prominent

.... Orchestra: limited variety of timbre

.... Sonority: tends toward a light, sparse sound

.... Tempo: fairly constant within a movement

Others: ....

ROMANTIC ELEMENTS OF STYLE

.... Melody of a lyric nature

.... Harmony: resolution of dissonance stressed

.... Orchestra: wide variety of timbre

.... Sonority: tends toward a rich, colorful sound

.... Tempo: fluctuates conspicuously within a movement

Others: ....

In the light of your analysis, this composition incorporates elements of the following styles: Check (✔)

.... New   .... Preromantic   .... Romantic

Study Guide 33

CHAPTER R96/S73

Respond to the incomplete and True-False statements with respect to American Jazz:

I. 1. T F Jazz is essentially an improvisational art.

2. Its musical elements contain influences derived from the cultures of ....
and from the .... musical tradition.

3. T F Our present popular music shows no African-American influence.

4. T F Jazz influences have permeated some of our concert and symphonic music.

5. T F Jazz performance permits improvisation on the part of one or several players at a time.

6. The term "jazz" was first applied around the year.. to a musical style evolved by black musicians in the city of ....

7. T F Since its inception, it has retained a consistently uniform style and character.

8. Two early idioms of New Orleans jazz were .... and ....

9. T F The blues is a native American musical and verse form with no known antecedents.

10. T F The blues has the character of a lament.

11. The blues stanza contains .... lines in which the ....
.... lines are identical.

12. Musically, the basic structure of the blues form contains .... measures.

13. "Bent" tones (vocal or instrumental deviations from standard pitch) are called ....
notes.

14. T F In general, the so-called blue notes are the lowered third, fifth, and seventh degrees of the scale.

15. Another common jazz form (of European origin) is the ....-bar
song form whose structure may be described with the letters ....

16. In performance, the modified restatements of the chorus constitute a series of ....

17. T F Simultaneous group improvisation results in a contrapuntal texture. (Ex.: *Dead Man Blues*.)

18. New Orleans style of performance is also known as ....

19. .... is a term first associated with the rhythmic momentum of
Louis Armstrong's style.

20. T F Duke Ellington's music is characterized by a close integration of the composed and the improvised.

21. T F Jazz instrumentation leans predominantly on wind and percussion instruments.

22. T F Jazz is essentially an art that finds its expression in solo and/or small ensemble performance.

23. T F The large and highly organized bands of the 1930s excluded the solo performer.

Notes

Part Eight

THE NEW MUSIC

Study Guide 34

CHAPTER R97/S74

I. Match each of the following items to its appropriate association with respect to twentieth-century movements in the arts:

Abstract Expressionism   Cubism   Dadaism   Environmental Art

Futurism   Pop Art   Surrealism

1. .... Originated in Italy; aspired to an "art of noises" that foreshadowed the advent of electronic music

2. .... Irreverence for traditional art and an inclination toward the absurd

3. .... Artistic expression based on the subconscious and the distorted images of the world of dreams

4. .... Geometric patterns substituted for the representation of realistic images

5. .... Space, mass and color freed from the need to imitate objects in the real world

6. .... Themes and techniques drawn from the world of commercial art

7. .... Involvement of the spectator as part of the art work

II. Complete the following with respect to trends in music in the mid-twentieth century:

1. John Cage, in his desire to expand musical resources, declared all .... as material proper to music.

2. The extension of the tone-row principle to elements of music other than pitch is called ....

3. Indeterminate music resulting from chance is called ....

4. Three devices used in the creation of electronic music are:

    a) ....   b) ....   c) ....

III. Check (✔) the true statements:

1. .... In aleatory music, the performer may be directed to choose for himself the order in which sections may be played.

2. .... Early experiments in France with tape recording as a compositional process were called *musique concrète*.

3. .... The synthesizer is restricted to a limited variety of sounds.

4. .... Electronic music can be created independent of traditional performing media.

5. .... Composers have avoided combining electronic music with live music.

6. .... In electronic music, dynamics and timbre acquire equal importance with pitch and rhythm.

7. .... Electronic devices facilitate the use of microtonal intervals.

8. .... In the new music, the area of articulation is expanded far beyond traditional practice.

9. .... Electronic music is international in scope.

IV. A tendency that seeks to combine techniques of contemporary music with those of jazz is called .... music. (p.R613/S445)

AURAL ANALYSIS
Stylistic Evaluation (Twentieth Century)

Schuller: *SEVEN STUDIES ON THEMES OF PAUL KLEE*

Or another of your choice.

Instructions:

1. Familiarize yourself with the evaluation outline.

2. Listen to the composition for general impression.

3. Listen again and complete the outline. Entries may be made during the listening process.

Composer .... Composition ....

Check (✔) the attributes that are prominently displayed in this composition with respect to the stylistic elements in each of the following categories:

NEW ELEMENTS OF STYLE

.... Melody of an unlyric nature

.... Harmony predominantly dissonant

.... Rhythm a dominating factor; frequent changes of meter

.... Prominence of percussiveness

.... Electronically generated sound

.... Serial technique

.... Jazz influence

.... Others: ....

PREROMANTIC ELEMENTS OF STYLE

.... Rhythm: regular meters predominate

.... Contrapuntal texture prominent

.... Orchestra: limited variety of timbre

.... Sonority: tends toward a light, sparse sound

.... Tempo: fairly constant within a movement

.... Others: ....

ROMANTIC ELEMENTS OF STYLE

.... Melody of a lyric nature

.... Harmony: resolution of dissonance stressed

.... Orchestra: wide variety of timbre

.... Sonority: tends toward a rich, colorful sound

.... Tempo: fluctuates conspicuously within a movement

.... Others: ....

In the light of your analysis, this composition incorporates elements of the following styles: Check (✔)

.... New   .... Preromantic   .... Romantic

AURAL ANALYSIS
Twentieth Century

Penderecki: *THRENODY FOR THE VICTIMS OF HIROSHIMA*

This composition is scored for fifty-two stringed instruments: 24 violins, 10 violas, 10 cellos, 8 double basses.

Instructions:

1. Listen to the composition for general impression.

2. Listen again and complete the outline. Entries may be made during the listening process.

Check ($\checkmark$) the statements that are relevant to this work:

I. 1. .... Unrelieved dissonant sounds

2. .... Strong sense of tonality prevails

3. .... Glissandos a prominent feature

4. .... Instruments used consistently in traditional manner

5. .... Instruments subjected to percussive treatment

6. .... Silence a significant factor in the overall scheme

7. .... Extreme pitch range exploited

8. .... Dynamic range limited

9. .... Thickly massed sounds in extreme registers

10. .... Indeterminate pitches contribute to the "art of noises"

II. 1. .... In terms of sound, this is conventional music

2. .... In terms of sound, the total effect approximates the character of electronic music

AURAL ANALYSIS
Electronic Music

Babbitt: *ENSEMBLES FOR SYNTHESIZER*

Or another of your choice.

Instructions:

1. Listen to the composition for general impression.

2. Listen again and complete the outline. Entries may be made during the listening process.

Composer ....   Composition ....

Check (✔) the musical qualities that are predominently displayed in this work:

Rhythm: .... Regular patterns in balanced relationship

                 .... Continually varied patterns

Meter: .... Recurrent regular pulse

                 .... No regular pulse

Tempo: .... Variable within the composition

                 .... Constant within the composition

                 .... Sounds projected at ultra-high speed

Pitch: .... Moderate range

                 .... Extreme range

Dynamics: .... Moderate range

                 .... Extreme range

Melody: .... Lyrical lines

                 .... Disjunct and fragmentary lines

Texture: .... Contrapuntal lines

                 .... No contrapuntal lines

Sonority: .... Light and sparse

                 .... Thickly massed sound

Electronic music, while sharing common elements with conventional music, creates a quality of sound beyond the traditional.   .... Yes

                 .... No

AURAL ANALYSIS
Stylistic Evaluation (Twentieth Century)

Composer .... Composition ....

Check (✔) the attributes that are prominently displayed in this composition with respect to the stylistic elements in each of the following categories:

NEW ELEMENTS OF STYLE

.... Melody of an unlyric nature

.... Harmony predominantly dissonant

.... Rhythm a dominating factor; frequent changes of meter

.... Prominence of percussiveness

.... Electronically generated sound

.... Serial technique

.... Jazz influence

.... Others: ....

PREROMANTIC ELEMENTS OF STYLE

.... Rhythm: regular meters predominate

.... Contrapuntal texture prominent

.... Orchestra: limited variety of timbre

.... Sonority: tends toward a light, sparse sound

.... Tempo: fairly constant within a movement

.... Others: ....

ROMANTIC ELEMENTS OF STYLE

.... Melody of a lyric nature

.... Harmony: resolution of dissonance stressed

.... Orchestra: wide variety of timbre

.... Sonority: tends toward a rich, colorful sound

.... Tempo: fluctuates conspicuously within a movement

.... Others: ....

In the light of your analysis, this composition incorporates elements of the following styles: Check (✔)

.... New   .... Preromantic   .... Romantic

Study Guide 35

CHAPTER R98/S75

Match each composer in the following list with the appropriate statement:

Babbitt	Boulez	Cage	Carter	Dallapiccola
Messiaen	Penderecki	Schuller	Stockhausen	Xenakis

1. .... A leading representative of the "third stream" movement
   (1925-   )

2. .... A Polish composer whose avant-garde procedures achieve the effect of
   (1933-   ) electronic sounds with conventional instruments

3. .... His *Three Compositions for Piano* (1947) and *Composition for Four In-*
   (1916-   ) *struments* (1948) were the first examples of total serialization

4. .... His special contribution to contemporary music involves a novel approach
   (1908-   ) to tempo which he calls "metrical modulation"

5. .... A worldwide spokesman for the antirational view of music
   (1912-   )

6. .... An Italian who unites his native vocal lyricism with the twelve-tone tech-
   (1904-   ) niques of the Viennese school

7. .... His theories about rhythm led the way to the incorporation of rhythm as a
   (1908-   ) factor within the serial process

8. .... A French composer-conductor; a leading advocate of total serialism
   (1925-   )

9. .... A German composer identified with the field of electronic, aleatory, and
   (1928-   ) serial music

10. .... A Greek composer whose unusual sound effects in *Pithoprakta* have been
    (1922-   ) a source of inspiration to composers of the Polish school

BIOGRAPHICAL SKETCH

Composer ....

His Life

Born (Year and Country) .... Died (Year and Country) ....

Places and people identified with his career:

....

....

....

....

Significant aspects of his career and styles: ....

....

....

....

....

....

....

....

....

....

His Music

1. Survey the composer's output as treated in the text and *underline* the relevant areas in the following list:

Ballet

Cantata

Chamber Music:

  Duo Sonata

  Octet

  Quartet

  Quintet

  Septet

  Sextet

  Solo Sonata

  Trio Sonata

Concerto

Concerto Grosso

Concert Overture

Electronic Music

Incidental Music

Jazz

Keyboard Music
  (organ, harpsichord, piano)

Madrigal

Mass

Motet

Opera

Oratorio

Orchestral Composition
  (category unspecified)

Passion

Song

Suite (orchestral)

Suite (solo)

Symphonic Poem

Symphony

Vocal Composition
  (category unspecified)

Others not listed: ....

APPENDIX

Bar references to Listening Guides and Aural Analysis Outlines.

Study Guide numbers are in roman type; bar numbers are in italics.

1. NUTCRACKER SUITE, Tchaikovsky
   March: 1-*1*; 2-*41*; 3-*49*. Dance of the Sugar-Plum Fairy: 1-*5*; 2-*9*; 3-*32*.
   Arab Dance: 1-*5*; 2-*14*; 3-*20, 31*; 4-*33*; 5-*69, 78, 86*. Chinese Dance: 1-*1*; 2-*3*.
   Dance of the Toy Flutes: 1-*3*; 2-*11, 27*; 3-*43*; 4-*62*.
   Waltz of the Flowers: 1-*1*; 2-*16*; 3-*34*; 4-*54*; 5-*70*; 6-*70*; 7-*86*; 8-*118*; 9-*134*; 10-*150*; 11-*164*; 12-*180*; 13-*196*;
       14-*218*; 15-*266*.

2. OVERTURE-FANTASY: *ROMEO AND JULIET*, Tchaikovsky
   1-*1*; 2-*11, 28*; 3-*41*; 4-*51*; 5-*78*; 6-*97*; 7-*112*; 8-*126*; 9-*143*; 10-*164*; 11a-*184*; 11b-*193*; 12-*213*; 13-*243*; 14-*273-
   344*; 15-*345*; 16-*353*; 17-*368*; 18-*446*; 19-*483*; 20-*485*; 21-*494*; 22-*508, 510*; 23-*518*.

3. SYMPHONY NO. 9, IN E MINOR, OPUS 95 (*From the New World*) (First movement), Dvořák
   1a-*1*; 1b-*6*; 2a-*9*; 2b-*13*; 3a-*16*; 3b-*22*; 4a-*24*; 4b-*28*; 5a-*39*; 5b-*63*; 6a-*91*; 6b-*107*; 6c-*125*; 7a-*149*; 7b-*171*; 8-*177*;
   9-*257*; 10a-*273*; 10b-*277*; 11-*288*; 12a-*312*; 12b-*328*; 12c-*354*; 13a-*370*; 13b-*392*; 14-*396*.

4. VIOLIN CONCERTO (First Movement), Mendelssohn
   1-*3*; 2-*25*; 3-*48*; 4-*73*; 5-*131*; 6-*139*; 7-*169*; 8-*210*; 9-*227*; 10a-*279*; 10b-*290*; 11-*298*; 12-*323*; 13-*336*; 14a-*352*;
   14b-*364*; 15a-*377*; 15b-*385*; 16-*414*; 17-*459*; 18-*473*.

5. SYMPHONY NO. 41 IN C MAJOR, K. 551 ("Jupiter") (First movement), Mozart
   1-*1*; 2-*9*; 3-*24*; 4-*37*; 5-*56*; 6-*81*; 7-*101*; 8-*121*; 9-*123*; 10-*133*; 11-*161*; 12-*171*; 13-*181*; 14-*189*; 15-*197*; 16-*212*;
   17-*225*; 18-*244*; 19-*269*; 20-*289*.

6. SYMPHONY NO. 40, IN G MINOR, K. 550 (First movement), Mozart
   1-*2*; 2-*21*; 3-*42*; 4-*44*; 5-*71*; 6-*73*; 7-*95*; 8-*101*; 9-*160*; 10-*165*; 11-*191*; 12-*225*; 13-*227*; 14-*259*; 15-*261*.

7. PIANO QUINTET IN A MAJOR, OPUS 114 ("Trout") (Fourth movement), Schubert
   1-*1*; 2-*21*; 3-*41*; 4-*61*; 5-*81*; 6-*101*; 7-*128*

8. SYMPHONY NO. 94, IN G MAJOR (*Surprise*) (Second movement), Haydn
   1-4-*1*; 5-6-*33*; 7-8-*49*; 9-*70*; 10-12-*75*; 13-16-*106*; 17-*139*; 18-*145*.

9. SYMPHONY No. 35, IN D MAJOR, K. 385 ("Haffner") (Third movement), Mozart
   1-*1*; 2-*1*; 3-*9*; 4-*17*; 5-*9*; 6-*25*; 7-*25*; 8-*33*; 9-*45*; 10-*33*; 11-*1*.

10. EINE KLEINE NACHTMUSIK, K. 525 (Third movement), Mozart
    1-*1*; 2-*1*; 3-*9*; 4-*9*; 5-*17*; 6-*17*; 7-*25*; 8-*17*; 9-*25*; 10-*1*.

11. PIANO SONATA IN C MINOR, Opus 13 ("Pathétique") (Third movement), Beethoven
    1-*1*; 2-*18*; 3-*25*; 4-*44*; 5-*62*; 6-*79*; 7-*121*; 8-*134*; 9-*154*; 10-*171*; 11-*182*.

12. HORN CONCERTO IN E-FLAT MAJOR, K. 447 (Third movement), Mozart
    1-*1*; 2-*9*; 3-*32*; 4-*34*; 5-*71*; 6-*77*; 7-*92*; 8-*98*; 9-*149*; 10-*155*.

13. MESSIAH, Handel
    Overture: 1-*1*; 2-*13*; 3-*95*. *He was despised:* 2-*1*; 3-*50*.
    Amen: 1-*1*; 2-*6*; 3-*11*; 4-*16*; 5-*20*; 6a-*21*; 6b-*26*; 7-*31*; 8-*36*; 9-*38*; 10-*42*; 11-*51*; 12a-*63*; 12b-*68*; 12c-*72*; 13a-*77*;
        13b-*85*; 13c-*86*.

NAME .... CLASS .... DATE ....

BIOGRAPHICAL SKETCH

Composer ....

His Life

Born (Year and Country) .... Died (Year and Country) ....

Places and people identified with his career:

....

....

....

....

Significant aspects of his career and styles: ....

....

....

....

....

....

....

....

....

....

....

....

His Music

1. Survey the composer's output as treated in the text and *underline* the relevant areas in the following list:

Ballet	Concerto	Opera
Cantata	Concerto Grosso	Oratorio
Chamber Music:	Concert Overture	Orchestral Composition (category unspecified)
Duo Sonata	Electronic Music	Passion
Octet	Incidental Music	Song
Quartet	Jazz	Suite (orchestral)
Quintet	Keyboard Music (organ, harpsichord, piano)	Suite (solo)
Septet	Madrigal	Symphonic Poem
Sextet	Mass	Symphony
Solo Sonata	Motet	Vocal Composition (category unspecified)
Trio Sonata		

Others not listed: ....

BIOGRAPHICAL SKETCH

Composer ....

His Life

Born (Year and Country) .... Died (Year and Country) ....

Places and people identified with his career:

....

....

....

....

Significant aspects of his career and styles: ....

....

....

....

....

....

....

....

....

....

His Music

1. Survey the composer's output as treated in the text and *underline* the relevant areas in the following list:

Ballet	Concerto	Opera
Cantata	Concerto Grosso	Oratorio
Chamber Music:	Concert Overture	Orchestral Composition
Duo Sonata	Electronic Music	(category unspecified)
Octet	Incidental Music	Passion
Quartet	Jazz	Song
Quintet	Keyboard Music	Suite (orchestral)
Septet	(organ, harpsichord, piano)	Suite (solo)
Sextet	Madrigal	Symphonic Poem
Solo Sonata	Mass	Symphony
Trio Sonata	Motet	Vocal Composition
		(category unspecified)

Others not listed: ....

BIOGRAPHICAL SKETCH

Composer ....

His Life

Born (Year and Country) .... Died (Year and Country) ....

Places and people identified with his career:

....

....

....

....

Significant aspects of his career and styles: ....

....

....

....

....

....

....

....

....

....

....

....

His Music

1. Survey the composer's output as treated in the text and *underline* the relevant areas in the following list:

Ballet	Concerto	Opera
Cantata	Concerto Grosso	Oratorio
Chamber Music:	Concert Overture	Orchestral Composition (category unspecified)
Duo Sonata	Electronic Music	
Octet	Incidental Music	Passion
Quartet	Jazz	Song
Quintet	Keyboard Music (organ, harpsichord, piano)	Suite (orchestral)
Septet		Suite (solo)
Sextet	Madrigal	Symphonic Poem
Solo Sonata	Mass	Symphony
Trio Sonata	Motet	Vocal Composition (category unspecified)

Others not listed: ....

BIOGRAPHICAL SKETCH

Composer ....

His Life

Born (Year and Country) .... Died (Year and Country) ....

Places and people identified with his career:

....

....

....

....

Significant aspects of his career and styles: ....

....

....

....

....

....

....

....

....

His Music

1. Survey the composer's output as treated in the text and *underline* the relevant areas in the following list:

Ballet	Concerto	Opera
Cantata	Concerto Grosso	Oratorio
Chamber Music:	Concert Overture	Orchestral Composition (category unspecified)
Duo Sonata	Electronic Music	
Octet	Incidental Music	Passion
Quartet	Jazz	Song
Quintet	Keyboard Music	Suite (orchestral)
Septet	(organ, harpsichord, piano)	Suite (solo)
Sextet	Madrigal	Symphonic Poem
Solo Sonata	Mass	Symphony
Trio Sonata	Motet	Vocal Composition (category unspecified)

Others not listed: ....

BIOGRAPHICAL SKETCH

Composer ....

His Life

Born (Year and Country) .... Died (Year and Country) ....

Places and people identified with his career:

....

....

....

....

Significant aspects of his career and styles: ....

....

....

....

....

....

....

....

....

....

His Music

1. Survey the composer's output as treated in the text and *underline* the relevant areas in the following list:

Ballet	Concerto	Opera
Cantata	Concerto Grosso	Oratorio
Chamber Music:	Concert Overture	Orchestral Composition (category unspecified)
Duo Sonata	Electronic Music	Passion
Octet	Incidental Music	Song
Quartet	Jazz	Suite (orchestral)
Quintet	Keyboard Music (organ, harpsichord, piano)	Suite (solo)
Septet	Madrigal	Symphonic Poem
Sextet	Mass	Symphony
Solo Sonata	Motet	Vocal Composition (category unspecified)
Trio Sonata		

Others not listed: ....

BIOGRAPHICAL SKETCH

Composer ....

His Life

Born (Year and Country) .... Died (Year and Country) ....

Places and people identified with his career:

....

....

....

....

Significant aspects of his career and styles: ....

....

....

....

....

....

....

....

....

....

....

His Music

1. Survey the composer's output as treated in the text and *underline* the relevant areas in the following list:

Ballet	Concerto	Opera
Cantata	Concerto Grosso	Oratorio
Chamber Music:	Concert Overture	Orchestral Composition
Duo Sonata	Electronic Music	(category unspecified)
Octet	Incidental Music	Passion
Quartet	Jazz	Song
Quintet	Keyboard Music	Suite (orchestral)
Septet	(organ, harpsichord, piano)	Suite (solo)
Sextet	Madrigal	Symphonic Poem
Solo Sonata	Mass	Symphony
Trio Sonata	Motet	Vocal Composition
		(category unspecified)

Others not listed: ....

NAME .... CLASS .... DATE ....

ABSOLUTE MUSIC ANALYSIS
Eighteenth-Nineteenth Centuries

Composition .... Composer ....

1. Identify the compositional type (such as sonata, symphony, concerto, suite, fugue, etc.) : ....

2. Indicate the number of movements and the structural design of each movement considered. Number of movements: ....

FORM

1st movement: .... 4th movement: ....

2nd movement: .... 5th movement: ....

3rd movement: .... 6th movement: ....

3. Check (✔) the attributes that are prominently displayed in this movement:

Melody: .... Extended line(s) of a marked lyrical nature

.... Moderately lyrical

Dynamics: .... Wide range; exploitation of extremes

.... Moderate range predominates

Pitch: .... Wide range; exploitation of extremes

.... Moderate range predominates

Timbre: .... Wide variety

.... Moderate variety

Sonority: .... Tends toward a rich, colorful sound

.... Tends toward a light, sparse sound

Tempo: .... Fluctuates conspicuously within a movement

.... Fairly constant within a movement

Expressive content: .... Projected by the materials of music within a relatively moderate range

.... Projected by the materials of music within a relatively expanded range

4. This composition is representative of the .... period.

5. With respect to this period, list other stylistic attributes that may be present in this composition.

....

....

....

151

ABSOLUTE MUSIC ANALYSIS
Eighteenth-Nineteenth Centuries

Composition .... Composer ....

1. Identify the compositional type (such as sonata, symphony, concerto, suite, fugue, etc.) : ....

2. Indicate the number of movements and the structural design of each movement considered. Number of movements: ....

FORM

1st movement: .... 4th movement: ....

2nd movement: .... 5th movement: ....

3rd movement: .... 6th movement: ....

3. Check (✔) the attributes that are prominently displayed in this movement:

Melody: .... Extended line(s) of a marked lyrical nature

.... Moderately lyrical

Dynamics: .... Wide range; exploitation of extremes

.... Moderate range predominates

Pitch: .... Wide range; exploitation of extremes

.... Moderate range predominates

Timbre: .... Wide variety

.... Moderate variety

Sonority: .... Tends toward a rich, colorful sound

.... Tends toward a light, sparse sound

Tempo: .... Fluctuates conspicuously within a movement

.... Fairly constant within a movement

Expressive content: .... Projected by the materials of music within a relatively moderate range

.... Projected by the materials of music within a relatively expanded range

4. This composition is representative of the .... period.

5. With respect to this period, list other stylistic attributes that may be present in this composition.

....

....

....

STYLISTIC EVALUATION
Baroque

Composition .... Composer ....

1. Check (✔) the attributes that are prominently displayed in this composition:

.... Basso continuo (bass line in continuous motion)

.... Basso ostinato

.... Continuous melodic expansion

.... Terraced dynamics

.... Persistent rhythmic drive

.... Single mood ("affection") per movement

.... The harpsichord a basic member of the orchestra

.... Contrapuntal texture predominates

.... Homophonic texture predominates

.... Duality of textures; contrapuntal and homophonic

.... Virtuosity a prominent factor

.... Lyricism a prominent factor

.... Embellishments abundantly present

.... Vocal music: frequent repetition of words and phrases

.... Vocal music: word-tone painting

2. With respect to this period, list other stylistic attributes that may be present in this composition:

....

....

....

STYLISTIC EVALUATION
Baroque

Composition .... Composer ....

1. Check (✔) the attributes that are prominently displayed in this composition:

.... Basso continuo (bass line in continuous motion)

.... Basso ostinato

.... Continuous melodic expansion

.... Terraced dynamics

.... Persistent rhythmic drive

.... Single mood ("affection") per movement

.... The harpsichord a basic member of the orchestra

.... Contrapuntal texture predominates

.... Homophonic texture predominates

.... Duality of textures; contrapuntal and homophonic

.... Virtuosity a prominent factor

.... Lyricism a prominent factor

.... Embellishments abundantly present

.... Vocal music: frequent repetition of words and phrases

.... Vocal music: word-tone painting

2. With respect to this period, list other stylistic attributes that may be present in this composition:

....
....
....

AURAL ANALYSIS
Stylistic Evaluation (Twentieth Century)

Instructions:

1. Familiarize yourself with the evaluation outline.

2. Listen to the composition for general impression.

3. Listen again and complete the outline. Entries may be made during the listening process.

Composer .... Composition ....

Check (✔) the attributes that are prominently displayed in this composition with respect to the stylistic elements in each of the following categories:

NEW ELEMENTS OF STYLE

.... Melody of an unlyric nature

.... Harmony predominantly dissonant

.... Rhythm a dominating factor; frequent changes of meter

.... Prominence of percussiveness

.... Electronically generated sound

.... Serial technique

.... Jazz influence

.... Others: ....

PREROMANTIC ELEMENTS OF STYLE

.... Rhythm: regular meters predominate

.... Contrapuntal texture prominent

.... Orchestra: limited variety of timbre

.... Sonority: tends toward a light, sparse sound

.... Tempo: fairly constant within a movement

.... Others: ....

ROMANTIC ELEMENTS OF STYLE

.... Melody of a lyric nature

.... Harmony: resolution of dissonance stressed

.... Orchestra: wide variety of timbre

.... Sonority: tends toward a rich, colorful sound

.... Tempo: fluctuates conspicuously within a movement

.... Others: ....

In the light of your analysis, this composition incorporates elements of the following styles: Check (✔)

.... New   .... Preromantic   .... Romantic

AURAL ANALYSIS
Stylistic Evaluation (Twentieth Century)

Composer .... Composition ....

Check (✔) the attributes that are prominently displayed in this composition with respect to the stylistic elements in each of the following categories:

NEW ELEMENTS OF STYLE

.... Melody of an unlyric nature

.... Harmony predominantly dissonant

.... Rhythm a dominating factor; frequent changes of meter

.... Prominence of percussiveness

.... Electronically generated sound

.... Serial technique

.... Jazz influence

.... Others: ....

PREROMANTIC ELEMENTS OF STYLE

.... Rhythm: regular meters predominate

.... Contrapuntal texture prominent

.... Orchestra: limited variety of timbre

.... Sonority: tends toward a light, sparse sound

.... Tempo: fairly constant within a movement

.... Others: ....

ROMANTIC ELEMENTS OF STYLE

.... Melody of a lyric nature

.... Harmony: resolution of dissonance stressed

.... Orchestra: wide variety of timbre

.... Sonority: tends toward a rich, colorful sound

.... Tempo: fluctuates conspicuously within a movement

.... Others: ....

In the light of your analysis, this composition incorporates elements of the following styles: Check (✔)

.... New   .... Preromantic   .... Romantic